Assessment Using the MMPI–2–RF is a practical guide that will be of huge value to students and experienced test users alike. As a seasoned personality assessment researcher and instructor, McCord is uniquely qualified to write this concise introduction to the MMPI–2–RF, highlighting the paradigm shift in assessment psychology reflected in its development, and offering detailed guidelines for administration, scoring, and interpretation of the inventory.

—**Yossef S. Ben-Porath, PhD,** Professor of Psychological Sciences, Kent State University, Kent, OH

This book presents an important shift in MMPI–2–RF interpretation by emphasizing the hierarchically organized dimensional structure of the MMPI–2–RF and provides an empirically supported interpretive framework, allowing readers to build a clinically useful and relevant report. The practical application of a dimensionally driven MMPI–2–RF interpretation is consistent with empirically driven models of psychopathology and represents a cutting-edge integration of contemporary theory in clinical practice. This guide will be widely used by instructors of graduate-level applied personality assessment as well as psychologists conducting MMPI–2–RF-based assessments in clinical and forensic settings.

—**Paul A. Arbisi, PhD, ABAP, ABPP, LP,** Staff Clinical Psychologist, Minneapolis VA Health Care Center; Professor, Department of Psychiatry and Adjunct Professor, Department of Psychology, University of Minnesota, Minneapolis

McCord has written a succinct, organized, and very user-friendly guide on how to interpret the MMPI–2–RF. It clearly elucidates the organizational framework of the instrument, which will be helpful to those getting started and a breath of fresh air to seasoned MMPI users otherwise accustomed to deciphering overly complicated interpretive schemes. Graduate students and practicing mental health professionals will benefit greatly from this book!

—**Martin Sellbom, PhD,** University of Otago, Dunedin, New Zealand

This accessible resource will be very helpful for those learning about and beginning to use the MMPI–2–RF, particularly graduate students in clinical and counseling psychology programs.

—**Dustin B. Wygant, PhD,** Associate Professor of Psychology and Director of Clinical Training, Eastern Kentucky University, Richmond

Assessment Using the MMPI–2–RF

Psychological Assessment Series

Assessment Using the MMPI–2–RF
David M. McCord

Assessment Using the Rorschach Inkblot Test
James P. Choca and Edward D. Rossini

Psychological Assessment Series

Assessment Using the MMPI–2–RF

David M. McCord

AMERICAN PSYCHOLOGICAL ASSOCIATION
Washington, DC

Published by
American Psychological Association
750 First Street, NE
Washington, DC 20002
www.apa.org

APA Order Department
P.O. Box 92984
Washington, DC 20090-2984
Phone: (800) 374-2721; Direct: (202) 336-5510
Fax: (202) 336-5502; TDD/TTY: (202) 336-6123
Online: http://www.apa.org/pubs/books
E-mail: order@apa.org

In the U.K., Europe, Africa, and the Middle East, copies may be ordered from
Eurospan Group
c/o Turpin Distribution
Pegasus Drive
Stratton Business Park
Biggleswade Bedfordshire
SG18 8TQ United Kingdom
Phone: +44 (0) 1767 604972
Fax: +44 (0) 1767 601640
Online: https://www.eurospanbookstore.com/apa
E-mail: eurospan@turpin-distribution.com

Typeset in Meridien by Circle Graphics, Inc., Columbia, MD

Printer: Sheridan Books, Chelsea, MI
Cover Designer: Mercury Publishing Services, Inc., Rockville, MD

Library of Congress Cataloging-in-Publication Data
Names: McCord, David Mark, author.
Title: Assessment using the MMPI–2–RF / David M. McCord.
Description: Washington, DC : American Psychological Association, [2018] |
Series: Psychological assessment series | Includes bibliographical references and index.
Identifiers: LCCN 2017030584 | ISBN 9781433828072 | ISBN 1433828073
Subjects: LCSH: Minnesota Multiphasic Personality Inventory.
Classification: LCC BF698.8.M5 M155 2018 | DDC 155.2/83—dc23 LC record available at https://lccn.loc.gov/2017030584

British Library Cataloguing-in-Publication Data
A CIP record is available from the British Library.

Printed in the United States of America
First Edition

http://dx.doi.org/10.1037/0000074-000

10 9 8 7 6 5 4 3 2 1

Contents

LIST OF FIGURES, TABLES, EXHIBITS, AND INTERPRETATION GUIDELINES *vii*

ABOUT THE SERIES *xi*

ACKNOWLEDGMENTS *xiii*

INTRODUCTION *3*

1. Overview of the MMPI–2–RF: History, Development, and Psychometric Considerations *7*
2. Administration and Scoring *19*
3. Description and Interpretation of the Protocol Validity Scales *29*
4. Description and Interpretation of the Substantive Scales *45*
5. Interpretive Framework *77*
6. Case Example *89*
7. Concluding Comments *111*

GLOSSARY *115*

REFERENCES *121*

INDEX *127*

ABOUT THE AUTHOR *139*

List of Figures, Tables, Exhibits, and Interpretation Guidelines

Figures

Figure 1.1 Psychopathology Assessment Model Used by the MMPI–2–RF *8*

Figure 6.1 Score Report *91*

Figure 6.2 MMPI–2–RF Interpretation Worksheet *99*

Tables

Table 1.1 Psychopathology Scales of the Minnesota Multiphasic Personality Inventory—2—Restructured Form by Domain *15*

Table 3.1 Interpretation of Cannot Say *(CNS)* Scores *31*

Table 3.2 Interpretation of Variable Response Inconsistency *(VRIN-r)* Scores *32*

Table 3.3 Interpretation of True Response Inconsistency *(TRIN-r)* Scores *33*

Table 3.4 Interpretation of Infrequent Responses *(F-r)* Scores *34*

Table 3.5 Interpretation of Infrequent Psychopathology Responses *(Fp-r)* Scores *35*

Table 3.6 Interpretation of Infrequent Somatic Responses *(Fs)* Scores *36*

Table 3.7 Interpretation of Symptom Validity *(FBS-r)* Scores *37*

Table 3.8 Interpretation of Response Bias Scale *(RBS)* Scores *38*

Table 3.9 Interpretation of Uncommon Virtues *(L-r)* Scores *39*

Table 3.10 Interpretation of Adjustment Validity *(K-r)* Scores *40*

Table 5.1 Interpretive Framework for Approaching the Test Data *78*

Exhibits

Exhibit 6.1 Example of a Full Narrative Report Composed by Transferring Interpretations From the Interpretation Worksheet *109*

Interpretation Guidelines

Somatic Complaints *(RC1)* Scores *47*
Malaise *(MLS)* Scores *47*
Gastrointestinal Complaints *(GIC)* Scores *48*
Head Pain Complaints *(HPC)* Scores *48*
Neurological Complaints *(NUC)* Scores *49*
Cognitive Complaints *(COG)* Scores *50*
Emotional/Internalizing Dysfunction *(EID)* Scores *51*
Demoralization *(RCd)* Scores *52*
Suicidal/Death Ideation *(SUI)* Scores *53*
Helplessness/Hopelessness *(HLP)* Scores *53*
Self-Doubt *(SFD)* Scores *54*
Inefficacy *(NFC)* Scores *54*
Low Positive Emotions *(RC2)* Scores *55*
Introversion/Low Positive Emotionality–Revised *(INTR-r)* Scores *56*
Dysfunctional Negative Emotions *(RC7)* Scores *56*
Stress/Worry *(STW)* Scores *57*
Anxiety *(AXY)* Scores *58*
Anger Proneness *(ANP)* Scores *58*
Behavior-Restricting Fears *(BRF)* Scores *59*
Multiple Specific Fears *(MSF)* Scores *60*
Negative Emotionality/Neuroticism–Revised *(NEGE-r)* Scores *60*
Thought Dysfunction *(THD)* Scores *62*
Ideas of Persecution *(RC6)* Scores *62*
Aberrant Experiences *(RC8)* Scores *63*
Psychoticism–Revised *(PSYC-r)* Scores *64*
Behavioral/Externalizing Dysfunction *(BXD)* Scores *65*
Antisocial Behavior *(RC4)* Scores *66*
Juvenile Conduct Problems *(JCP)* Scores *67*

Substance Abuse *(SUB)* Scores *68*
Hypomanic Activation *(RC9)* Scores *68*
Aggression *(AGG)* Scores *69*
Activation *(ACT)* Scores *70*
Aggressiveness–Revised *(AGGR-r)* Scores *70*
Disconstraint–Revised *(DISC-r)* Scores *71*
Family Problems *(FML)* Scores *72*
Cynicism *(RC3)* Scores *73*
Interpersonal Passivity *(IPP)* Scores *74*
Social Avoidance *(SAV)* Scores *74*
Shyness *(SHY)* Scores *75*
Disaffiliativeness *(DSF)* Scores *76*

About the Series

To conduct a thorough and informative psychological assessment, practitioners need to master a complex set of skills that go beyond the rote procedures laid out in a test manual. The Psychological Assessment Series features brief, practical books by veteran practitioners who synthesize their professional wisdom into expert tips and insights for conducting a wide range of educational and psychological assessments. Each book provides context for using a specific test, including the history of its development and its current uses, followed by recommendations on when to use the test and how to combine it with other assessment tools. Also included are step-by-step instructions for administration, advice for navigating challenging scenarios, and guidance on how to use or adapt the test for a particular population of clients or, for example, when diagnosing a specific disorder, evaluating personality traits, and monitoring treatment or other interventions. All volumes in this series can be used as both educational tools for graduate students in assessment courses and handy references for practitioners. Each book can be paired with a companion video that features the author demonstrating the assessment process in real time, followed by an analysis that highlights significant moments from the demonstration along with key takeaways. The books and videos may be used independently, but together they make an ideal learning tool for students and trainees.

Acknowledgments

I am heavily indebted to the authors of the Minnesota Multiphasic Personality Inventory—2—Restructured Form, Yossef S. (Yossi) Ben-Porath and Auke Tellegen. They have been extraordinarily supportive and encouraging over the years, to me personally as well as to countless numbers of my students. Bev Kaemmer of the University of Minnesota Press has played an important role in all of our lives. More specifically, Yossi and Bev took time to carefully review and critique the first draft of this book, and they generously provided permission to use the significant amount of copyrighted material contained here. I also want to warmly acknowledge the constructive relationships I have enjoyed with other members of the community of researchers on the Minnesota Multiphasic Personality Inventory, including Nathan Weed, Martin Sellbom, Paul Arbisi, Jack Graham, John McNulty, Allan Harkness, Mike Bagby, Dustin Wygant, Anthony Tarescavage, Jacob Finn, Ryan Marek, Adam Hicks, and many more, including my own current and former students. Finally, I would like to express my gratitude to Linda Malnasi McCarter and her colleagues at the American Psychological Association (including Resarani Johnson, Ed Meidenbauer, and David Becker) for providing such a positive publication experience, from beginning to end.

Assessment Using the MMPI–2–RF

Introduction

The Minnesota Multiphasic Personality Inventory—2—Restructured Form (MMPI–2–RF) represents a fundamental change in how we conceptualize and assess personality and psychopathology. The old paradigm, on which the original MMPI was based, consists of a set of discrete categorical diagnoses that a client or patient either has or doesn't have. The new paradigm conceptualizes psychopathology as a hierarchical structure of dimensional constructs ranging from relatively broad to relatively narrow in scope. The Research Domain Criteria project, introduced around 2010 by the National Institute of Mental Health (Insel, 2014), operationalizes this new paradigm, as do the several variants of five-factor models currently guiding research in the field of psychopathology. The MMPI–2–RF both reflects and contributes to this major paradigm shift.

In the context of the new paradigm, the MMPI–2–RF provides accurate measurement of 40 dimensional constructs related to personality and psychopathology (with an additional nine scales measuring protocol validity, or the individual's test-taking approach). These 40 constructs are arranged in three vertical tiers (broad, midlevel, and narrow) spanning five content domains: (a) Somatic/Cognitive, (b) Internalizing, (c) Thought Dysfunction, (d) Externalizing, and (e) Interpersonal Functioning. This book describes a two-pass approach to interpreting the MMPI–2–RF.

---

http://dx.doi.org/10.1037/0000074-001
Assessment Using the MMPI–2–RF, by D. M. McCord

The first pass is a top-down scan of the data, considering the broadest constructs first (Internalizing, Thought Dysfunction, and Externalizing). Next are nine midlevel scales that provide information about key factors within each of the five domains. Finally, the narrowest level includes facets of the midlevel scales. This quick first look provides an overall orientation to the client or patient with regard to key broad areas of difficulty as well as more specific issues that may be critical (e.g., suicidality). The second pass is a left-to-right examination of the results by each domain in turn, beginning, as noted above, with the Somatic/Cognitive Scales and ending with the Interpersonal Functioning Scales. The first pass is a quick overview, taking 4 or 5 minutes usually, and the second pass is the detailed interpretation step, using tools and guidelines presented in this book.

The MMPI was the first psychological test that really worked, and since about 1940 it has been ranked Number 1 in terms of use by clinical psychologists. The MMPI was so successful in the clinical world that both practitioners and scholars resisted updating or revising it for almost 50 years. The transition to the MMPI–2 (Butcher, Dahlstrom, Graham, Tellegen, & Kaemmer, 1989) was successful as, beyond restandardization, the changes really were not that dramatic. However, the paradigm shift that was introduced with the Restructured Clinical (RC) Scales in 2003 and then fully implemented with the publication of the MMPI–2–RF in 2008 was significant, and it was a controversial and disruptive issue in the field of psychological assessment for almost a decade. A full presentation of the early criticisms of the restructured instrument is beyond the scope of this book, and the various criticisms and point-by-point rebuttals by the test developers and supporters are widely available in the assessment journals, particularly in the 2006–2007 time period. An excellent summary of the key criticisms and responses to those criticisms is presented in Ben-Porath's (2012a) article on the use of the MMPI–2–RF in high-stakes forensic settings.

The basic assumption of this book is that the paradigm has now shifted, the hierarchical–dimensional model has replaced the categorical model, and future revisions of the MMPI will essentially fine-tune the current restructured form, such as by expanding the set of constructs covered while retaining the basic structure. Indeed, the similarly restructured adolescent version of the test, the Minnesota Multiphasic Personality Inventory—Adolescent—Restructured Form (MMPI–A–RF; Archer, Handel, Ben-Porath, & Tellegen, 2016), has recently been published.

The *MMPI–2–RF Manual for Administration, Scoring, and Interpretation* (Ben-Porath & Tellegen, 2008/2011) and the accompanying *MMPI–2–RF Technical Manual* (Tellegen & Ben-Porath, 2008/2011) are key sources of information for this book. Ben-Porath's (2012b) book *Interpreting the MMPI–2–RF* is a masterpiece of scholarship and is the key MMPI–2–RF resource for both researchers and practitioners. It is more than 500 pages in length, and it augments the test manuals with a thorough presentation of underlying historical and theoretical issues regarding personality, psychopathology, psychometrics, measurement theory, and controversies; it also includes extensive referencing of the empirical literature. The present book follows the intent of the American Psychological Association's Psychological Assessment Series, which is to provide an applied, practical guide to the use and interpretation of the MMPI–2–RF. The concept was that a book was needed for two key groups: (a) graduate students in applied psychology training programs and (b) practicing health care psychologists who want to add the MMPI–2–RF to their repertoire of tools.

Much of the substantive interpretive material in this book is drawn directly from the *MMPI–2–RF Manual for Administration, Scoring, and Interpretation* and *Interpreting the MMPI–2–RF*. Specifically, the text boxes presented in Chapters 3 and 4 are close copies of the text boxes in both of these primary sources (which are themselves identical in this regard). This mirroring is intentional and done with the permission and strong recommendation of the copyright holder and test authors. The interpretive statements were carefully developed on the basis of item content in some cases (content validity) and empirical correlates in others (criterion validity). The quality and consistency of MMPI–2–RF interpretations across psychologists are beneficial to clients and to the profession, and the use of these formal, "official" interpretive statements obviously supports optimum consistency.

Psychologists conducting the assessment and writing the report should also feel free to use these interpretive statements verbatim, without citing the source. This is not plagiarism but is actually the recommended practice for MMPI–2–RF interpretation. The computer-generated Score Report reproduced in Chapter 6 is included with permission of the copyright holder, as is the Interpretation Worksheet, also in Chapter 6. Finally, the stepwise interpretive framework presented in this book with only minor modifications was developed primarily by Yossef Ben-Porath and his graduate students at Kent State University.

Looking Ahead: Plan for the Book

The overview presented so far may feel more disorienting than helpful, but the assessment model will become clear as we proceed. Chapter 1 provides a brief overview of the MMPI–2–RF, describing the key issues in the development of the original MMPI and the transitions to the MMPI–2, the RC Scales, and ultimately the MMPI–2–RF itself. The chapter concludes with a quick review of the MMPI–2–RF's psychometric characteristics, highlighting key points to consider during scale interpretation. In Chapter 2, I cover standard practices with regard to administering and scoring the MMPI–2–RF. (Computer-based administration and scoring are strongly recommended.)

Actual scale interpretation begins in Chapter 3, with the Protocol Validity Scales. These scales are always examined first and address the client's approach to the task. The broad issues are responsiveness, consistency, tendency to overreport psychopathology, and tendency to underreport psychopathology. In Chapter 4, I cover all 42 of the Substantive Scales of the MMPI–2–RF, going in order of domain. The Somatic/Cognitive domain is first, with six scales, followed by Internalizing with 15 scales, Thought Dysfunction with four scales, Externalizing with nine scales, and Interpersonal Functioning with six scales; the two Interest Scales are briefly described at the end.

Chapter 5 is a formal presentation of the interpretive framework I will use, including the two-pass approach to the test results. As mentioned above, the first pass consists of a brief consideration of the Protocol Validity Scales and then an overview of the Substantive Scales, beginning with the broadest level, then the midlevel scales, and finally the narrow-band scales. This pass provides a general orientation to a set of results. The second pass is slower and more systematic, and I will guide readers through each of the five major domains, extracting interpretive statements from Chapter 4 and adding them to the Interpretation Worksheet. The Substantive Scales and interpretation text boxes in Chapters 3 and 4 are presented in parallel order to the Interpretation Worksheet, which greatly facilitates this step in the process. The information accumulating on the Interpretation Worksheet, which will include, in addition to interpretive statements, notes regarding diagnostic and treatment implications, will ultimately be included in the final psychological report on the case. Finally, in Chapter 6, a case example is presented that provides a demonstration of the interpretive approach described in Chapter 5.

Again, the interpretation procedures advocated in this book are tightly aligned with the recommendations in the test user manual (Ben-Porath & Tellegen, 2008/2011) and in Ben-Porath's (2012b) book. Indeed, the specific interpretive information presented in the text boxes is virtually identical to that given in these basic sources. The interpretive framework presented in Chapter 5 is intended to promote reliability and consistency in MMPI–2–RF interpretation, from case to case and across examiners. The narrative interpretation of a set of MMPI–2–RF scores should be a reflection of the scores themselves, not the particular psychologist doing the interpretation. Close adherence to the procedures described will enhance the quality of MMPI–2–RF interpretation in applied settings as well as the consistency of test interpretation, which then promotes public confidence in the validity of psychological assessment.

How to Use This Book

This book is intended to be primarily a practical guide or handbook that is used as a key to interpretation each time the MMPI–2–RF is administered. More specifically, it is likely that readers will read the Introduction along with Chapters 1 and 2 just once, referring back to them only rarely. Chapters 3 and 4 provide the "official" interpretive statements for specific ranges of test scores, and thus these chapters are desktop tools that readers can use in every case. The interpretation steps described in Chapter 5, using the case example in Chapter 6, typically become internalized within the first dozen or so cases, and readers may review them only occasionally.

In addition to this book, readers should use the Interpretation Worksheet, an interactive tool available at no cost from the University of Minnesota website (Regents of the University of Minnesota, 2012), in every case. The steps described in Chapter 5 are based on examining the protocol data systematically by domain, drawing appropriate interpretive narratives from Chapters 3 and 4, typing them into the Interpretation Worksheet, and then cutting and pasting them from the worksheet into the final comprehensive psychological report. Readers will also find it useful to download a sample report from the Pearson website and to print it out for easy reference while going through Chapter 5 (Pearson, 2014). These and links to other MMPI–2–RF resources are available on the companion website (http://pubs.apa.org/books/supp/mccord).

Overview of the MMPI–2–RF

History, Development, and Psychometric Considerations

1

The Minnesota Multiphasic Personality Inventory (MMPI) is the most widely used self-report measure of personality and psychopathology in history, a status it has sustained throughout its 75-year existence. The current version of the test, the MMPI–2—Restructured Form (MMPI–2–RF), is now used in psychological and psychiatric outpatient and inpatient settings, in general as well as specialized medical settings (e.g., prescreening for spinal surgery or bariatric procedures), in a variety of forensic psychology settings, and in employment screening in certain high-impact occupations such as police officer. It is also the most widely researched; for all versions of the MMPI, the total number of peer-reviewed, published research papers approaches 20,000.

The MMPI–2–RF is composed of 338 true–false test items that form 51 separate scales. As noted in the Introduction, nine of these scales assess protocol validity, allowing for a thorough assessment of the text taker's attitude and approach to taking the test, and two of the scales represent broad vocational and personal interest patterns. The remaining 40 scales are substantive measures of personality and psychopathology. These 40 scales target specific dimensional constructs and are arranged (vertically) in a hierarchical structure, ranging in scope from relatively broad to relatively narrow (see Figure 1.1). The Substantive Scales are organized (horizontally) into

http://dx.doi.org/10.1037/0000074-002
Assessment Using the MMPI–2–RF, by D. M. McCord

FIGURE 1.1

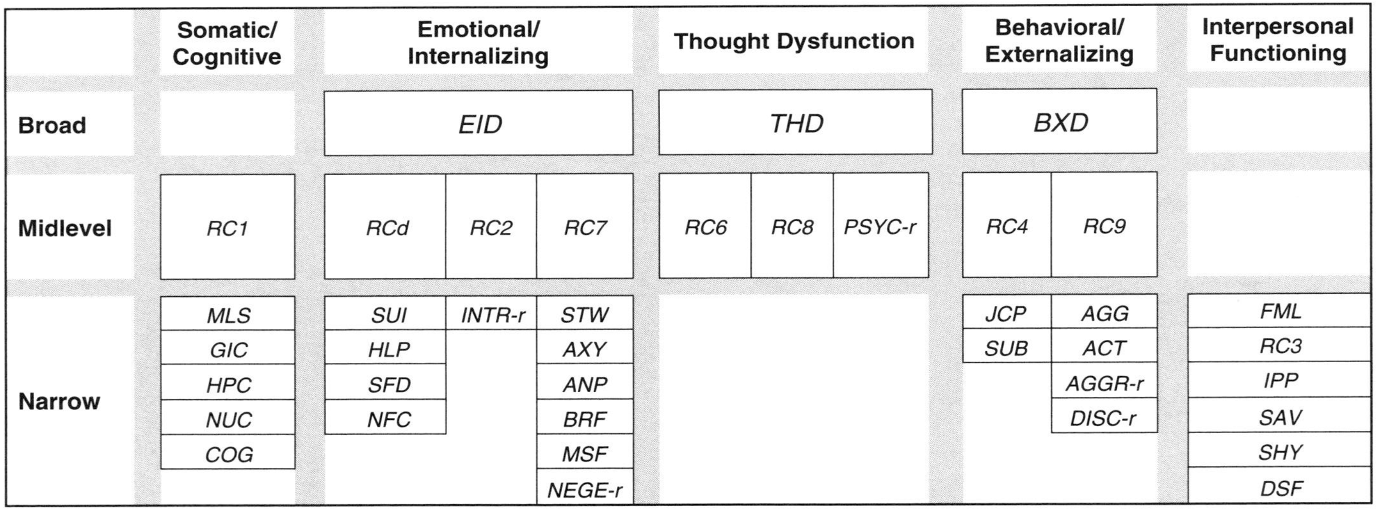

	Somatic/ Cognitive	Emotional/ Internalizing			Thought Dysfunction			Behavioral/ Externalizing		Interpersonal Functioning
Broad		*EID*			*THD*			*BXD*		
Midlevel	*RC1*	*RCd*	*RC2*	*RC7*	*RC6*	*RC8*	*PSYC-r*	*RC4*	*RC9*	
Narrow	*MLS*	*SUI*	*INTR-r*	*STW*				*JCP*	*AGG*	*FML*
	GIC	*HLP*		*AXY*				*SUB*	*ACT*	*RC3*
	HPC	*SFD*		*ANP*					*AGGR-r*	*IPP*
	NUC	*NFC*		*BRF*					*DISC-r*	*SAV*
	COG			*MSF*						*SHY*
				NEGE-r						*DSF*

Psychopathology assessment model used by the MMPI–2–RF. *RC1* = somatic complaints; *MLS* = malaise; *GIC* = gastrointestinal complaints; *HPC* = head pain complaints; *NUC* = neurological complaints; *COG* = cognitive complaints; *EID* = emotional/internalizing dysfunction; *RCd* = demoralization; *SUI* = suicide/death ideation; *HLP* = helplessness/hopelessness; *SFD* = self-doubt; *NFC* = inefficacy; *RC2* = low positive emotions; *INTR-r* = introversion/low positive emotions; *RC7* = dysfunctional negative emotions; *STW* = stress/worry; *AXY* = anxiety; *ANP* = anger proneness; *BRF* = behavior-restricting fears; *MSF* = multiple specific fears; *NEGE-r* = negative emotionality/neuroticism; *THD* = thought dysfunction; *RC6* = ideas of persecution; *RC8* = aberrant experiences; *PSYC-r* = psychoticism; *BXD* = behavioral externalizing dysfunction; *RC4* = antisocial behavior; *JCP* = juvenile conduct problems; *SUB* = substance abuse; *RC9* = hypomanic activation; *AGG* = aggression; *ACT* = activation; *AGGR-r* = aggressiveness; *DISC-r* = disconstraint; *FML* = family problems; *RC3* = cynicism; *IPP* = interpersonal passivity; *SAV* = social avoidance; *SHY* = shyness; *DSF* = disaffiliativeness. Excerpted from the *MMPI–2–RF Manual for Administration, Scoring, and Interpretation*, by Yossef S. Ben-Porath and Auke Tellegen.

five content domains, three of which link clearly to historical and widely accepted conceptualizations of psychopathology: Internalizing (with 15 scales assessing constructs related to anxiety and depression), Thought Dysfunction (with four scales assessing constructs such as delusions and hallucinations), and Externalizing (with nine scales assessing constructs such as aggression and substance use). In addition, six scales assess the Somatic/Cognitive domain (e.g., malaise, cognitive complaints), and six scales assess the Interpersonal Functioning domain (e.g., cynicism, shyness). This new paradigm approach results in a remarkably comprehensive profile of the test taker's characteristics and supports a systematic, reliable, and accurate method of test interpretation. The following sections briefly review the origins of the MMPI circa 1940, the restandardization and other changes that resulted in the MMPI–2 in 1989, the introduction of the Restructured Clinical (RC) Scales in 2003, and the publication of the full MMPI–2–RF in 2008.

Early History of the MMPI

Starke Hathaway, a research psychologist, and J. C. McKinley, chief of neurology, both at the University of Minnesota Hospitals, sought to develop an omnibus test instrument that would identify the presence of any of the major clinical syndromes used during the 1935–1940 period. Their first formal publication was in 1940 (Hathaway & McKinley, 1940). Psychiatric diagnosis at that time was based on Kraepelinian categories that had evolved to reflect psychodynamic theoretical constructs to varying degrees (for a more extensive discussion, see Ben-Porath, 2012b). The initial diagnostic categories were Hypochondriasis, Depression, Hysteria, Psychopathic Deviate, Paranoia, Psychasthenia, Schizophrenia, and Hypomania. Subsequently, the Masculinity–Femininity and Social Introversion Scales were added, resulting in the 10 Clinical Scales that formed the core measures of the test until the Restructured Form was published in 2008.

Briefly, Hathaway and McKinley collected a large set of more than 1,000 items that was intended to be inclusive of all major symptoms of these syndromes. They reduced this list to just more than 500 items through rational judgment and then administered the items to the group of 724 "Minnesota Normals" as well as sets of patients exhibiting the specific pathology at hand (the criterion groups). It should be noted that the Minnesota Normals group consisted primarily of individuals in the hospital waiting room who were visiting family or friends; this group was almost entirely White, was primarily Protestant, had an average education of eighth grade, was largely rural, and primarily worked on farms or in blue-collar employment.

A hallmark feature of the MMPI was the use of the relatively new method of "empirical keying," rather than item content, to determine which items should form a specific scale: Items that exhibited a true–false proportion in the criterion group that differed significantly from the true–false proportion in the normative group were identified as members of the Clinical Scale for that syndrome. The 10 scales were thus formed, with item counts ranging from 33 to 78; these were long scales with heterogeneous content, as each scale tended to capture all items that distinguished that particular criterion group from the normative group. The 724 Minnesota Normals who served as the comparison group for item selection also served as the standardization group (for the next 50 years!), providing the means and standard deviations by which raw scores were converted to standardized linear *T* scores to indicate a test taker's relative elevation on a given scale.

Hathaway's original concept was that incoming patients would complete the test, and the result would ideally be a single spike indicating which one of the 10 diagnostic groups they should be placed in. He did not formally deny that a person could have more than one disorder, but he expected that most were struggling with a single, specific disorder that would be indicated by a single elevation. The test never actually worked in this way, as multiple elevations occurred more often than not, and MMPI interpretation very soon became focused on pattern analysis ("code types") rather than individual scale scores. For readers interested in this earliest phase of the MMPI's development, a unique volume is available, an edited work by Welsh and Dahlstrom (1956) that includes all published articles on the test by 1956, plus a number of articles written specifically for that volume that had not been otherwise published.

By around 1960, the test had generated thousands of publications, most of which were descriptions of narrowly focused empirical or technical studies. There was a growing need for more clinically oriented, user-friendly, practical guidebooks to supplement the abundant technical information. Early classics of historic significance are books by Dahlstrom and Welsh (1960) and Dahlstrom, Welsh, and Dahlstrom (1972, 1975). Two very important MMPI scholars, Jack Graham and Roger Greene, added to this line with their own handbooks, which have been updated regularly through the years. See Graham (1977) for the first entry in his series and Graham (2011) for the most recent, as well as Greene's (2011) most recent version. It should be noted that throughout the decades, many additional specific scales and coherent sets of scales have been developed to augment clinical interpretation beyond the standard Protocol Validity and Clinical Scales. These include the Content Scales, Content Component Scales, and Personality Psychopathology Five (PSY–5) Scales, as well as a wide variety of stand-alone scales generally labeled the Supplementary Scales. The guidebooks by Graham and Greene provide excellent coverage of these additional scales, and the most recent editions cited above include the transition to the MMPI–2–RF. Another recent comprehensive text covering both the MMPI–2 and MMPI–2–RF was authored by Friedman, Bolinskey, Levak, and Nichols (2015).

Development of the MMPI–2

As noted above, the original normative group for the MMPI was a sample of convenience, primarily individuals in the waiting rooms of the University of Minnesota hospitals who had accompanied friends or relatives to the facility. These 724 individuals were astonishingly homogeneous by today's standards. Almost all were rural Minnesotans who were White, Protestant (predominantly Lutheran), of Scandinavian descent, and with an average eighth-grade education. By the 1980s, the serious inadequacy of this comparison group, given the international and highly diverse applications of the MMPI, was sorely apparent. Nevertheless, there was great resistance to the idea of altering the test in any way, as it had been the first clearly successful instrument of its type.

Ultimately, the decision was made to provide new and representative norms and to update the test at the item level (through additions, deletions, and rewording) but, because of the vast empirical database on code-type interpretation, to keep the 10 traditional Clinical Scales intact. The Restandardization Committee consisted of James Butcher, Grant Dahlstrom, Jack Graham, Auke Tellegen, and Beverly Kaemmer of the University of Minnesota Press. The decision to leave the Clinical Scales unaltered had significant positive and negative effects. On the positive side, this decision placated the very large population of MMPI users who had become skilled in code-type interpretation with the existing scales despite the psychometric flaws. The continuity of the Clinical Scales was reassuring to the user base and facilitated a relatively rapid transition to the MMPI–2 (1989) and a phasing out of the original MMPI by the publisher within a very few years. The negative effects of this decision are addressed in the sections that follow.

Development of the Restructured Clinical Scales

The decision to leave the Clinical Scales intact through the 1989 restandardization was a strategic one, designed to ease the transition and retain the MMPI user base. Unfortunately, this decision extended the life span of some major psychometric problems with the original scales that were increasingly visible and understood by MMPI researchers. A group led by Auke Tellegen and Yossef Ben-Porath, ultimately including John McNulty, Paul Arbisi, Jack Graham, and Bev Kaemmer, engaged in a multiyear project aimed at restructuring the Clinical Scales and dealing with the underlying flaws.

The empirical keying method used by Hathaway had allowed extensive item overlap across scales, a practice usually avoided by modern test makers. The existence of a common factor of psychopathology was discussed in the literature and identified as "demoralization" by the research group. Hathaway's technique had captured this common element to some degree on every scale, which contributed to excessive cross-scale correlations. The use of a single scale to measure a complex clinical syndrome had resulted in remarkably heterogeneous content in many of the scales, creating yet more measurement problems. The RC Scales include a specific measure of the common factor demoralization (Demoralization *[RCd]*), which has been statistically removed (as needed) from the other eight RC Scales. These restructured forms of the original scales have been dramatically shortened and focused on relatively unidimensional constructs intended to reflect the "major distinctive core" of the original scale. The most detailed description of the restructuring of the Clinical Scales is provided in a test monograph published by the University of Minnesota Press, available on both the Press and Pearson websites (Tellegen et al., 2003).

Development of the MMPI–2–RF

Five years after the introduction of the RC Scales, the full MMPI–2–RF was published. The MMPI–2–RF consists of 338 of the original 567 items in the MMPI–2. Thus, MMPI–2–RF profiles can be extracted from MMPI–2 data sets, which has been a boon for researchers. The RC Scales include a single, focused measure of demoralization, and the additional eight RC Scales are psychometrically improved unidimensional measures of the major distinctive core constructs of the original parent scales. The development process resulted in focused and psychometrically strong primary scales, but many important facets of clinical syndromes had been removed from these scales. Thus, the test developers spent the next several years identifying important concepts beyond demoralization and the major distinctive core constructs, ultimately producing an instrument with 51 scales. There are nine Protocol Validity Scales, three Higher-Order Scales, nine RC Scales, 23 Specific Problems Scales, two Interest Scales, and five PSY–5 Scales.

Paradigm Shift From Categorical to Dimensional Diagnosis

What is not immediately evident in the sequential history described thus far is that a major paradigm change occurred in the basic conceptualization of psychopathology. This new perspective is critically important to understanding and effectively using the MMPI–2–RF (and future versions of the test). Briefly, as noted in the Introduction, the historic model of psychopathology is essentially *categorical*—that is, various "mental disorders" are seen as relatively discrete entities or syndromes, with a variety of symptoms serving as clues to a hypothetical single underlying disorder, and an individual can be judged as having or not having this disorder. Categorical, dichotomous thinking regarding psychopathological phenomena is evident from early human history, such as in Hippocrates' "types" of mental disorders, and it was formalized by the German nosologist Emil Kraepelin in the early 1920s. The Kraepelinian diagnostic system included many of the syndrome names still familiar, such as Schizophrenia, Manic Depression, and Hysteria, and this system served explicitly as the foundation for the original MMPI scales as well as for the subsequent diagnostic systems in the *Diagnostic and Statistical Manual of Mental Disorders (DSM)* and the *International Classification of Diseases* (ICD). Categorical thinking is embedded deeply in modern culture. We typically think of people as "having" attention-deficit/hyperactivity disorder, posttraumatic stress disorder, major depressive disorder, or autism spectrum disorder. Even the current writing standard of people-first language (e.g., individuals with autism, people with schizophrenia), although certainly more sensitive and preferable, perpetuates the discrete categorical conceptualization of psychological dysfunction.

The alternative conceptual framework is to view psychopathological phenomena as *dimensional*—that is, as ranging from low to high, with the low end possibly in the "normal" range of functioning. This rethinking is very easy to see with some key psychopathology constructs such as anxiety; we all know people who are characteristically low in anxiety, others who tend to be high, and many who are in between. Similarly, it is easy to see the underlying dimensionality in the distribution of constructs like shyness, boldness, depressivity, self-efficacy, independence, energy level, and so forth. Some of these constructs may in fact follow a relatively normal, bell-shaped distribution in the population, whereas others may be ordinal but not normally distributed, and still others may show abrupt "steps" and threshold effects suggesting underlying genetic mechanisms. This new paradigm for conceptualizing psychopathology may be succinctly described as a hierarchical organization of dimensional constructs ranging from relatively broad to relatively narrow in scope.

The debate over whether psychopathology is best seen as categories (taxa) versus dimensions (continua) has gone on for many decades, and the MMPI has been at the center of it. Ben-Porath (2012b) provided a thorough discussion of this issue. Although the original Clinical Scales were developed on the basis of the association of item endorsement with membership in categorical diagnostic groups, more recent additions to the MMPI–2, particularly, were clearly dimensional. Specifically, the Content Scales (Butcher, Graham, Williams, & Ben-Porath, 1990) were based on the identification of relatively focused, homogeneous constructs, with scale scores interpretable throughout their range. The theoretically important PSY–5 Scales (Harkness, McNulty, & Ben-Porath, 1995) represent a hierarchical model of dimensional constructs spanning the broad spectrum of personality and psychopathology. Following Harkness and McNulty's earlier work (see, e.g., Harkness & McNulty, 1994), current hierarchical–dimensional models of psychopathology now include those described by Kotov et al. (2011), Krueger (1999), and Watson, Kotov, and Gamez (2006), among others.

The move away from categorical models in favor of hierarchical–dimensional models has been energized by strategic planning within the National Institute of Mental Health (NIMH). The NIMH Strategic Plan of 2010 (Insel, 2014) explicitly acknowledged the failure of the traditional categorical diagnostic system reflected by the *DSM* and ICD to produce benefits in terms of general improvements in the lives of people, with no significant changes in the rates of most major psychological problems over the past several decades. The strategic plan called for abandoning the current diagnostic system in favor of a hierarchical–dimensional model that incorporated emerging knowledge from neurobiology, including genetic advances, and technological advances in areas such as digital imaging. The specific framework NIMH proposed, the Research Domain Criteria (RDoC) project, was offered as a framework to guide research, and in 2013 NIMH boldly stipulated that research proposals that used *DSM* diagnostic categories as variables of interest would not be considered for funding (see Insel, 2013). Although this stance was softened somewhat, the message was clear, and the RDoC initiative has had a major impact in shifting psychopathology research away from categorical diagnostic conceptualizations.

As I have noted, the MMPI was evolving in parallel, from a straightforward categorical framework originally, with dimensional elements added gradually, to a fully hierarchical–dimensional system with the MMPI–2–RF. This model is presented in Figure 1.1 and Table 1.1 in order to provide a preview of the framework I present in detail in subsequent chapters. As noted above, the MMPI–2–RF has 51 scales; nine of these are protocol validity measures, and two are measures of general interest patterns. The remaining 40 scales measure personality and psychopathology constructs. Figure 1.1 depicts the hierarchical structure of these 40 scales, using acronyms rather than full scale names due to space constraints; the full scale names are presented in Table 1.1, arranged by domains to make it easy to visually link the acronyms to the scale names.

The purpose of Figure 1.1 is to emphasize the organizational structure of the psychopathology constructs in the MMPI–2–RF assessment model. Vertically, there are three levels reflecting breadth of the construct, with three broad overarching scales, nine midlevel scales, and 28 relatively narrower scales. Horizontally, these constructs are organized into five domains. It is important to note that domains are not categories, and our goal is not to see into which domain a client falls. The client will have scores on all 40 scales, and our task is to organize the findings and describe the individual in a manner that is accurate, thorough, clear, and coherent and that can lead to meaningful recommendations. If Emotional/Internalizing Dysfunction *(EID)* is clinically elevated and is higher than the other two Higher-Order Scales (Thought Dysfunction *[THD]* and Behavioral/Externalizing Dysfunction *[BXD]*), and if a majority of individual scale elevations are within the Internalizing domain, then the narrative report is likely to start with that domain. However, there may well be elevations in other domains, such as Family Problems *(FML)* and perhaps Substance Abuse *(SUB)*, and these issues will certainly be addressed as well.

In summary, this new paradigm guides the approach to individual assessment taken in this book. We have a set of 40 well-constructed measures of dimensional personality and psychopathology constructs, organized hierarchically into domains based primarily on co-occurrence. Our task is to describe the individual as accurately as possible, fully acknowledging his or her uniqueness, rather than trying to determine into what category he or she should be placed. Although in reality it is often necessary to "code" our clients using the existing diagnostic system in order to comply with reimbursement processes and possibly to establish eligibility for support services, we serve our clients best by developing a thorough, accurate description first, fully recognizing their individuality.

Psychometric Considerations

The first set of scales I consider are the nine Protocol Validity Scales, plus an additional indicator, which is the count of omitted (or double-marked) items. These scales reflect the test taker's attitude and approach to the task itself. Three main questions are addressed. First, to what extent is the test taker responsive to the content of the

TABLE 1.1

Psychopathology Scales of the Minnesota Multiphasic Personality Inventory—2—Restructured Form by Domain

Domain	Scale	Abbreviation
Somatic/Cognitive	Somatic Complaints	*RC1*
	Malaise	*MLS*
	Gastrointestinal Complaints	*GIC*
	Head Pain Complaints	*HPC*
	Neurological Complaints	*NUC*
	Cognitive Complaints	*COG*
Internalizing	Emotional/Internalizing Dysfunction	*EID*
	Demoralization	*RCd*
	Suicidal/Death Ideation	*SUI*
	Helplessness/Hopelessness	*HLP*
	Self-Doubt	*SFD*
	Inefficacy	*NFC*
	Low Positive Emotions	*RC2*
	Introversion/Low Positive Emotionality–Revised	*INTR-r*
	Dysfunctional Negative Emotions	*RC7*
	Stress/Worry	*STW*
	Anxiety	*AXY*
	Anger Proneness	*ANP*
	Behavior-Restricting Fears	*BRF*
	Multiple Specific Fears	*MSF*
	Negative Emotionality/Neuroticism–Revised	*NEGE-r*
Thought Dysfunction	Thought Dysfunction	*THD*
	Ideas of Persecution	*RC6*
	Aberrant Experiences	*RC8*
	Psychoticism–Revised	*PSYC-r*
Externalizing	Behavioral/Externalizing Dysfunction	*BXD*
	Antisocial Behavior	*RC4*
	Juvenile Conduct Problems	*JCP*
	Substance Abuse	*SUB*
	Hypomanic Activation	*RC9*
	Aggression	*AGG*
	Activation	*ACT*
	Aggressiveness–Revised	*AGGR-r*
	Disconstraint–Revised	*DISC-r*
Interpersonal Functioning	Family Problems	*FML*
	Cynicism	*RC3*
	Interpersonal Passivity	*IPP*
	Social Avoidance	*SAV*
	Shyness	*SHY*
	Disaffiliativeness	*DSF*

Note. Excerpted from the *MMPI–2–RF Manual for Administration, Scoring, and Interpretation*, by Yossef S. Ben-Porath and Auke Tellegen.

items? Issues here are responsiveness in general (e.g., did he or she answer all questions?) and consistency of responses (evaluated by considering pairs of items with either similar or opposite content). Second, to what extent might the test taker be overreporting the level of psychopathology that is objectively present? Overreporting may be intentional or unintentional, and it may involve general psychopathology or specific sets of symptoms. Third, to what extent might the test taker be underreporting the level of psychopathology that is objectively present? Again, underreporting may be intentional or unintentional.

I then go through the five domains of psychopathology constructs. The Somatic/Cognitive domain includes six scales assessing physical, somatic, and cognitive complaints. These may be general (weakness, fatigue) or more specific (e.g., gastrointestinal complaints). The Internalizing domain includes the highest frequency symptoms and contains 15 scales, proportionally the largest category assessed by the test. These symptoms include constructs such as anxiety, fears and phobias, distress, unhappiness, suicidal thinking, anhedonia, self-doubt, and hopelessness. The Thought Dysfunction domain includes four scales measuring statistically the least frequent symptoms, those associated with psychotic conditions, including hallucinations and delusions. The nine scales of the Externalizing domain include measures of impulsivity, aggressiveness, hyperactivity, substance abuse, and other forms of antisocial behavior. Finally, the Interpersonal Functioning domain has six scales assessing various traits associated with the quantity and quality of interpersonal relationships (e.g., interpersonal passivity, shyness, cynicism, social avoidance).

Cutting across the five broad domains, the test authors have identified seven specific scales as having critical content that may suggest the need for immediate attention and action by the clinician. The Critical Scales are Suicidal/Death Ideation *(SUI)*, Helplessness/Hopelessness *(HLP)*, Anxiety *(AXY)*, Ideas of Persecution *(RC6)*, Aberrant Experiences *(RC8)*, Substance Abuse *(SUB)*, and Aggression *(AGG)*. When these scores are elevated, the computer-generated Score Report provides item-level information on the scales, which are indicated in bold font. Use of the Critical Scales is discussed in greater detail in Chapters 4, 5, and 6.

With a total of 51 scales, a detailed psychometrics analysis of reliability and validity is beyond the scope of this clinical handbook. These data are available in the *MMPI–2–RF Technical Manual* (Tellegen & Ben-Porath, 2008/2011). Specifically, the *Technical Manual* provides reliability estimates and standard errors of measurement for all scales based on the normative sample, as well as numerous well-defined clinical samples. There are numerous studies that report classification accuracy (sensitivity and specificity) using simulations or known-group research designs. The *Technical Manual* reports close to 40,000 correlation coefficients reflecting internal structure and consistency, as well as almost 54,000 correlation coefficients indicating association with external criteria.

At this time there are approximately 400 peer-reviewed empirical articles in the assessment literature supporting the validity of the MMPI–2–RF. A current bibliography of MMPI–2–RF research is constantly maintained by the University of Minnesota Press (2017). To summarize, the reliability data are very strong, the validity data (including construct validity, criterion validity, and predictive validity) are very strong, and the peer-reviewed literature is very strong. These claims are well supported by the primary and secondary references included in this book.

One final structural comment has to do with item overlap. As noted above, one source of excessive cross-scale correlations on the Clinical Scales of the MMPI and MMPI–2 was that in the original scale, development items were allowed to occur on multiple scales. The MMPI–2–RF is hierarchical, which complicates this issue to some extent. For example, an item that occurs on the narrowest level, such as Helplessness/Hopelessness *(HLP)*, might very logically also occur on its corresponding midlevel scale Demoralization *(RCd)* and then again on the Higher-Order Scale Emotional/Internalizing Dysfunction *(EID)*. However, item overlap was not allowed on scales within the same level of the hierarchy. Further, on this issue, the PSY–5 Scales are treated as an independent scale set. So, no items are shared among the three Higher-Order Scales, no items are shared across the nine RC Scales, and no items are shared across the 23 Specific Problems Scales. Although no items are shared across the five PSY–5 Scales themselves, items may co-occur between the PSY–5 Scales and scales at all three levels of the hierarchical structure. In the case example in Chapter 6, the client omitted just one of the 338 items (with content concerning marijuana use), yet this item occurred on Substance Abuse *(SUB)* at the most specific level, Antisocial Behavior *(RC4)* at the middle level, Behavioral/Externalizing Dysfunction *(BXD)* at the highest level, and Disconstraint–Revised *(DISC-r)* among the PSY–5 Scales.

Administration and Scoring

2

Self-report instruments are, unfortunately, often treated in a rather cavalier way by psychologists. In contrast, the guidelines for establishing rapport are essential and very clear, and the testing environments for instruments like the Wechsler tests and individually administered achievement tests are carefully structured. I strongly recommend that examiners treat the Minnesota Multiphasic Personality Inventory—2—Restructured Form (MMPI–2–RF) just as carefully as they would a Wechsler test with regard to establishing a working relationship with the client and then carefully adhering to the standardized administration procedures described in this chapter. Using standard procedures helps ensure that the resulting profile is representative of the test taker's individual characteristics rather than reflecting unique aspects of the testing situation. Standardized administration is especially important when interpretation is aided by the use of comparison groups (described below), as these groups were formed with the assumption of standardized administration procedures.

The MMPI–2–RF should be administered by a qualified professional or an assistant working under the direct supervision of the qualified professional. The full definition of *qualified professional* is presented in Chapter 2 of the *MMPI–2–RF Manual for Administration, Scoring, and Interpretation* (Ben-Porath & Tellegen, 2008/2011) and is briefly summarized here. The qualified professional must have graduate-level training in psychological testing and

http://dx.doi.org/10.1037/0000074-003
Assessment Using the MMPI–2–RF, by D. M. McCord

assessment and be familiar with basic psychometrics, including reliability, measurement error, various types of validity, norms, and the derivation of standard scores. The examiner should also have graduate training in psychopathology and personality. Training and supervised experience in administration, scoring, and interpretation of the MMPI–2 or the MMPI–2–RF are required. Appropriate administration of the MMPI–2–RF involves (a) consideration of whether the client possesses the suitable characteristics for testing with this instrument, (b) adherence to the standard modalities of administration and responding, and (c) use of standard administration instructions and procedures.

Client Issues Influencing Administration

AGE

The normative group consisted of individuals 18 and older. Individuals younger than 18 should not be given the MMPI–2–RF, although those who are 14 to 18 years old could be administered the adolescent form of the test (MMPI–A–RF; Archer, Handel, Ben-Porath, & Tellegen, 2016). Note that 18 is an overlap age: Test authors of both instruments agree, largely on the basis of experience with the MMPI–2 and MMPI–A, that 18-year-old individuals who are still living with their parents should be given the adolescent form of the test and those who are in college, working, or living on their own should be given the MMPI–2–RF. However, there are some suggestions, pending further research, that the MMPI–2–RF may overpathologize the profiles of 18-year-old respondents (Ben-Porath, 2012b), and this possibility should be considered in the interpretation of results.

HISTORY OF PRIOR TESTING

Taking the MMPI (any version) is a long and meaningful experience for most people, and it is helpful to have some sense of the client's previous experiences of assessment with the MMPI or other related tools to help correct any misconceptions or distorted expectations he or she may have. This issue should ideally be addressed early in the assessment encounter rather than directly preceding the MMPI–2–RF administration itself so as to minimize any direct impact on the results.

TESTABILITY OF THE CLIENT

The test is most often administered by computer or with a test booklet. Thus, essential requirements are that the test taker be able to see well, to read adequately, and to comprehend the meanings of the test items. The examiner likely has formal or informal data regarding these issues, including simple observation of the client's visual capabilities, academic history, and results of collateral testing in the current encounter. It is good practice, though, for examiners to explicitly consider these basic client capabilities as they begin the MMPI–2–RF administration. The reading level required for the MMPI instruments has been a focus of extensive research over the years, a review of which is beyond the scope of this practical handbook. The most current perspective is that the average technical reading level for the items is Grade 4.5, and the test authors recommend that the test not be administered when the test taker has a reading ability level below sixth grade. When technical reading level is adequate, comprehension may still be a problem in certain cases, such as when mental status problems are present or when the test taker is not a native English speaker. It should be noted that validated versions of the MMPI–2–RF are available in Spanish and in Canadian French.

Standard Administration Modalities

The MMPI–2–RF may be administered using a test booklet, a computer-presented version, or an official audio recording of the items. The audio version is available on CD and is also available within the computer software. It is not recommended that the examiner read the items aloud to the test taker, as this introduces obvious variation from the standard stimulus presentation and further introduces an interpersonal element that could impact the client's responses. When the booklet or audio version is used, the client responds using a pencil and a Scantron answer sheet (Scantron Corporation, Eagan, Minnesota). In the computer version, the 338 items are presented in the same order, one item at a time, and the client responds by clicking *true* or *false*. The computer version now supports iPad (Apple, Cupertino, California) administration as well, which is even easier for most clients.

For many reasons, the computer-administered version is strongly preferred. Equivalence with the paper form has been well established empirically. The response burden on the client is greatly reduced. The time of administration averages 25 to 35 minutes for the computer version versus 35 to 50 minutes for the booklet version. The computer format, with one item at a time on the screen and an easy click or touch on *true* or *false*, is much easier than going back and forth between an item booklet and a relatively dense Scantron sheet and then making sure the right bubble is being filled in. Hand entering raw answer sheet data into the software later is somewhat time consuming and error prone. Full hand scoring and manual plotting of profiles are even more time consuming and error prone.

In addition, computer administration allows immediate scoring, which is clinically beneficial for numerous reasons. The examiner has immediate access to the count of any omitted items and can instruct the client to return to those items and complete them. The availability of Critical Scales and items is readily visible to the examiner and can support rapid response as warranted. The inclusion of the full text of any critical items endorsed allows for an immediate, brief follow-up interview to determine what the client was thinking as he or she responded to each of those items. The newest and most sophisticated platform offered by Pearson Assessments (San Antonio, Texas) is Q-global, which is fully web based and centralized with regard to test inventory, case storage, and so forth. The only drawback is that active Internet access is required;

however, with Wi-Fi increasingly available, and especially with the low cost and ease of providing a personal hotspot by cell phone, it is a very rare assessment setting that could not accommodate this option. In such cases, the use of Pearson's Q Local platform, which is housed on an individual computer and does not require active Internet access, is recommended as an alternative way to obtain most of the advantages of computer-assisted testing.

Standard Administration Instructions and Procedures

The standardization sample was originally assessed using the booklet and paper form of the test, and test takers were given a very specific set of instructions. Thus, these instructions should always be used when administering the test. They are printed in the test booklet, in the computer administration, and in the test manual, but they are reproduced here as well, in that it is critically important to use these precise instructions:

> This inventory consists of numbered statements. Read each statement and decide if it is *true as applied to you* or *false as applied to you*.
>
> You are to mark your answers on the answer sheet you have. Look at the example of the answer sheet shown at the right. If a statement is **true** or **mostly true** as applied to you, blacken the circle marked **T**. If a statement is **false** or **not usually true** as applied to you, blacken the circle marked **F**. If a statement does not apply to you or if it is something that you don't know about, make no mark on the answer sheet. But try to give a response to every statement.
>
> Remember to give **your own** opinion of yourself.

In the middle paragraph of these instructions, the computer-administered version replaces the steps regarding marking the answer sheet with appropriate language regarding clicking or touching *true* or *false*.

As already noted, the MMPI–2–RF is a restricted clinical assessment instrument that should be administered by a qualified professional or an assistant directly supervised by a qualified professional. It is important for the examiner to be available and observant throughout the testing. The test authors suggest that it is not necessary for the examiner to be physically present and close at hand for the entire 25 to 35 minutes, and brief breaks are generally acceptable. However, for most of the time, the test taker should be within view of the examiner, and the examiner should be available to the test taker as questions or problems arise. The test should not be sent home with the client, and MMPI–2–RF test materials should always remain under appropriate professional control.

It is not unusual for clients to have questions about the procedures and about the meanings of specific items or terms. It is important to respond with variations on the standard instructions presented above and not to give clients any definitions or suggestions about how they might solve their problem with the test. Their responses should always reflect their own deliberations without any nonstandardized contributions from the examiner. Examiners' responses can be gentle, encouraging, and supportive, but not substantive. One of the most common sticking points for some clients has to do with the dichotomous choice; a commonly used encouraging response by the examiner is simply to repeat the key instruction, emphasizing the second phrase: "You should mark false if the item is '**false** or **not usually true** as applied to you.'" It is essential to maintain standardized conditions, and it is also essential to maintain a therapeutic alliance with clients. When they do not know the definition of a word, for example, it is fine for the examiner to apologize, to say that he or she would really like to help them, but the procedures for using this test do not allow the examiner to explain any of the items or define any words.

Another challenge for the examiner often arises in specific contexts in which external motivations exist for underreporting or overreporting psychopathology. The client may have his or her own personal agenda, and a personal goal of the examiner is to avoid ending up with a profile that violates the Protocol Validity indicators (described in Chapter 3, this volume). It is tempting to prepare clients with a strong lecture on the importance of being fully honest and neither exaggerating nor minimizing their personal issues. This type of response set guidance is appropriate only in a very general sense, as applying to all tests and procedures, and at the beginning of the assessment as part of the overall orientation. Further, specific coaching targeting the key MMPI–2–RF validity issues (consistency, overreporting, underreporting) should never be given; research evidence shows that specific guidance regarding validity indicators actually reduces their effectiveness (e.g., Bagby, Nicholson, Bacchiochi, Ryder, & Bury, 2002).

As with Wechsler and other major psychological tests, the assessment should take place in a quiet, distraction-free, physically comfortable environment. Individually administered testing is preferred. The MMPI–2–RF can be administered in groups, but the examiner should remain present and vigilant at all times (in case, for example, a test taker has questions, external distractions arise, or a test taker becomes disruptive and to maintain control over materials).

Scoring Options and Procedures

Briefly stated, a raw score must first be tabulated for each of the 51 scales of the MMPI–2–RF, and then the raw score must be converted to a standard score by comparing it with the scores of the normative group. This process can be achieved through hand scoring methods or by computer, and the latter is, again, very strongly recommended. Hand scoring involves the use of transparency templates that are placed on the answer sheet, and scorable responses are counted and written on a profile sheet. This process is both time consuming, requiring about 30 minutes even by an experienced examiner, and error prone. An intermediate solution is to hand enter the raw item true–false scores into the computer program, which gains the significant advantages of computer-generated report options (described later). Double entry is recommended for error reduction, which then takes 10 to 12 minutes on average. The ideal solution is to administer the test by computer, with automatic computer scoring.

NORMATIVE GROUP

Raw scores are converted to standardized scores by comparing the client's individual raw score on a scale to the mean and standard deviation of the normative group for that scale. The normative sample for the MMPI–2–RF is generally the same archival sample used in the development of the MMPI–2 (Butcher, Dahlstrom, Graham, Tellegen, & Kaemmer, 1989), with one difference: The MMPI–2 used separate norms for men ($n = 1{,}138$) and women ($n = 1{,}462$). For a number of reasons related to federal non-discrimination laws, nongendered norms were evaluated for the MMPI–2–RF and were found to be psychometrically acceptable. Thus, 1,138 women were drawn at random from the 1,462 so that gender groups would be of equal size, yielding a norm group of 2,276 men and women. This group exhibits characteristics that generally follow the 1990 census, with the acknowledgment of a slight overrepresentation of Whites and underrepresentation of Asians and Hispanics. Information regarding the rationale for nongendered norms, the psychometric findings supporting the use of nongendered norms, and extensive descriptive information regarding the MMPI–2–RF norm group itself may be found in several sources (Ben-Porath, 2012b; Ben-Porath & Tellegen, 2008/2011; Tellegen & Ben-Porath, 2008/2011).

DERIVATION OF STANDARD SCORES

In order to meaningfully understand a client's score on a scale, the raw score must be converted to a standard score reflecting the deviation from the mean of the normative group. For many personality and psychopathology measures, the *T* score has been the traditional choice, with a mean of 50 and standard deviation of 10. The original MMPI used a straightforward conversion formula to calculate the linear *T* score associated with a given raw score. The problem was that the psychopathology scale scores were not normally distributed in the population; they were significantly positively skewed, and to widely varying degrees. The result in practical terms was that a *T* score on one scale might reflect a very different percentile rank than the same *T* score on another scale, complicating interpretation.

With the development of the 1989 MMPI–2, a modification was adopted, labeled the *Uniform T score*. Very briefly, this metric preserves the positive skew of the raw score distributions, which is an accurate reflection of the distribution of these psychopathology constructs in the population, but equates the level of skewness. Thus, a Uniform *T* score reflects the same percentile rank, regardless of scale, based on the "average" positively skewed distribution across all scales in the given set. The Uniform *T* score has been used as well in the MMPI–2–RF, with the exception of the Protocol Validity Scales and the Interest Scales, as these have substantially different raw score distributions and use traditional linear *T* scores (see Ben-Porath, 2012b, for a more detailed discussion of this issue).

For the Substantive Scales, unless otherwise noted, a *T* score of 65 or higher is designated as being in the clinical range. The Protocol Validity Scales have varying cut points, and an increasing number of scales provide empirically validated interpretations for low scores and for score ranges other than a simple cut point for clinical significance at $T = 65$.

Report Options and Features

There are currently three different computer-generated report options available for the MMPI–2–RF, and there are other specialty reports in the development pipeline. Most commonly used is the Score Report, which provides scores on all 51 scales plus additional item-level information that highlights potentially high-impact responses. The case example presented in Chapter 6 includes a full Score Report. The Interpretive Report includes the Score Report and adds a computer-generated narrative interpretation. It should be noted that the Interpretive Report follows exactly the same framework and logic I present in Chapter 5; a skilled examiner who adheres carefully to the approach recommended in this book will produce a narrative report that is remarkably consistent with the computer-generated report. Finally, the Police Candidate Interpretive Report is a specialized score report that is designed specifically for evaluating police officer candidates.

SCORE REPORT

The Score Report is the standard and most commonly used report for the MMPI–2–RF. It is described here with reference to Figure 6.1 in Chapter 6, which reproduces the actual output. Page 1 of the report is a cover sheet that provides basic client data obtained at the time of testing. Page 2 is the first of five profile sheets and includes Cannot Say (*CNS*; a raw count) and all nine of the Protocol Validity Scales presented graphically. Page 3 is the second of five profile sheets and presents the Higher-Order Scales and the Restructured Clinical Scales. The third profile sheet, on page 4, presents the Specific Problems Scales in the Somatic/Cognitive and Internalizing domains, and the fourth profile sheet, on page 5, presents the Specific Problems Scales for the Externalizing and Interpersonal Functioning domains, as well as the two Interest Scales. Page 6 of the report exhibits the fifth profile sheet with the PSY–5 Scales.

Page 7 is an extremely useful reorganization of all of the scores that supports the second pass (detailed interpretation) of the two-pass interpretive strategy advocated in this volume. This page is titled "MMPI–2–RF T SCORES (BY DOMAIN)" (referred to in this book as the *scores-by-domain report*) and presents the scale scores in a framework that clearly exemplifies the hierarchical structure of the MMPI–2–RF assessment model. The five profile sheets include the same profiles in the same order that would be produced by hand scoring and hand plotting. The ordering of these profiles drives the first pass (orientation) of the two-pass interpretive approach.

The last page of the report, page 8, focuses on item-level information that helps the examiner quickly focus on potentially urgent concerns. Seven of the MMPI–2–RF scales have been identified by the test developers as having critical item content: Suicidal/Death Ideation *(SUI)*, Helplessness/Hopelessness *(HLP)*, Anxiety *(AXY)*, Ideas of Persecution *(RC6)*, Aberrant Experiences *(RC8)*, Substance Abuse *(SUB)*, and Aggression *(AGG)*. If the *T* score on any of these scales reaches 65 or higher, the full text of each item answered in the scored direction is printed on page 8 of the report, including the percentage of the norm group that answered that item in the scored direction. If the *SUI* score is elevated, it is shown in bold face. These data provide the examiner with potentially critical information that may warrant immediate intervention.

INTERPRETIVE REPORT

The Interpretive Report is a state-of-the-art example of computer-assisted psychological assessment. The Interpretive Report includes all sections of the Score Report described above and adds a computer-generated narrative interpretation. The Interpretive Report is not reproduced here for space reasons and also because some of its most advanced features do not translate to print. Specifically, each of the sentences in the narrative is tagged to its source, which may be a test response (face-valid item content), an empirical correlate, or an inference (by the test authors). A large proportion of the narrative statements are test responses or correlates, and this proportion is increasing as the volume of empirical research grows. Hovering the mouse pointer over a sentence produces a pop-up box that identifies the source (e.g., correlate) and the scale score that triggered the statement (e.g., *RC6* = 70).

Further, each statement has an endnote, and following the narrative is a list of endnotes that point to reference numbers for the empirical research articles that support the interpretive statement. Finally, the reference list itself is included, with active hyperlinks in many cases to the full text of the article cited. This aspect of the report is extremely valuable to any psychologist working in a forensic or other high-stakes setting as it provides extensive empirical support for specific test interpretations in a readily available format. It is recommended that the reader visit the Pearson Clinical Assessment website (http://www.pearsonclinical.com), search for MMPI–2–RF, click on the Scoring and Reporting tab, and then examine one or more of the sample Interpretive Reports.

USER-DESIGNATED ITEM-LEVEL INFORMATION

In all reports a listing of endorsed scorable items on seven Critical Scales is produced on page 8 when the *T* score on that scale reaches 65 or higher. All reports allow the user to customize this feature in two ways. First, the cutoff score of 65 may be modified to be higher or lower, which could be useful in specific clinical contexts. Second, other scales, with user-specified cutoffs, may be added optionally by the user to this section of the report. For example, for inpatient facilities to which individuals with bipolar-type dysfunction are typically referred, it may be helpful to check Hypomanic Activation *(RC9)* and Activation *(ACT)* as Critical Scales, in addition to the seven scales included automatically.

COMPARISON GROUPS

The standard scoring and profiling data are based on *T* scores derived from the full normative sample. Optionally, the user may select an additional comparison group that reflects a population or setting that is more specific to the client being assessed. The Pearson software includes a large and growing set of comparison groups from which to choose. At the time of this writing, there were 23 different comparison groups drawn from 18 different settings. Briefly, these include outpatient groups, inpatient groups, Veterans Affairs samples, medical samples (bariatric surgery candidates, spinal surgery candidates, chronic pain patients), forensic samples (disability claimants, custody litigants, sex offenders, inmates), college students, and college student counseling center samples, among others.

When the user designates a comparison group for a given assessment case, the comparison group data are represented in the profile graph along with the standard scoring data based on the normative sample. The client's scores across scales compared with the normative group are represented as solid circles connected by solid lines, and the means of the comparison group on each scale are shown with open diamonds connected by dashed lines. The standard deviations (±1) for the comparison group are shown by bars around the means. This may be seen in the example case in Chapter 6 (see page 2 of Figure 6.1), in which the College Counseling Clinic comparison group was used.

Additional information is also added to the numerical data presented below the profile graph. The standard information includes the client's raw scores, *T* scores, and percentage of items completed on each scale. When a comparison group is added, three additional lines show the mean and standard deviation for the comparison group for each scale, plus the percentage of the comparison group scoring at or below the test taker on that scale. Comparison group data are also added to the item-level information on the computer-generated reports (page 8). For each of the default seven scales plus any user-designated scales, when the client's score reaches the cutoff point, all endorsed scorable items are printed in full; the percentage of the normative sample responding in the same direction is indicated, and when a comparison group is selected, the percentage of that comparison group responding in the same direction is also listed.

The Pearson software now allows users to create their own custom comparison groups. Within the software, the user designates a name for the new comparison group and then identifies a minimum of 200 stored cases to be included in the group. The comparison group is then created and added to the drop-down list from which the user can choose in any given assessment case. Custom comparison groups may be exported and imported.

The Pearson software debits one usage (or charge) when an assessment is originally scored, and there is no additional cost to rescore the case subsequently. Thus, it is often helpful to score a test case in a standard manner, examine the results, and then rescore it using other comparison groups or user-designated item-level information.

Advantages of Computer-Assisted Administration and Scoring

For many reasons mentioned in the preceding sections, users of the MMPI–2–RF are strongly advised to implement computer-based processes for the administration and scoring of this instrument. Those reasons are summarized here.

The response burden on clients is lessened considerably, which arguably helps them stay fully attentive and engaged in the assessment process in general. The likelihood of error is essentially eliminated. The immediacy of results can substantially improve the timing and quality of intervention, particularly when urgent issues are revealed by test data. The level of detail in the computer-generated reports is substantially greater than would realistically be achieved in manual scoring; the very tedious hand-scoring procedure for Variable Response Inconsistency *(VRIN-r)* and True Response Inconsistency *(TRIN-r)*, tempting the busy practitioner to omit these very important scales, and the inclusion of the percentage of items completed for each of the 51 scales, which is a much more useful indication of nonresponsiveness than the simple overall *CNS* score, are details few if any clinicians would normally tabulate by hand. Standard item-level information and then user-designated item-level information are readily available and can be extremely useful. The use of comparison groups adds substantially to the interpretation of a client's scores. The reorganization of scores presented on the scores-by-domain report (page 7 of the Score Report) greatly facilitates the process of integrating test findings into the comprehensive narrative report of the assessment.

All of the features described thus far are available in the basic Score Report. Although the cost of this report is not trivial, a careful consideration of the time and effort involved on the part of the client and certainly the examiner suggests that manual processing likely saves little, if any, cost.

The Interpretive Report is, of course, a more significant investment of resources. It may well be worthwhile in busy settings in which the examiner could certainly apply the interpretive strategy presented in Chapter 5 and thus produce a highly similar interpretation, but having the computer assist in the process saves time that can be productively used otherwise. In high-stakes settings, including those potentially involving litigation, the annotation features of the Interpretive Report are invaluable. Having clear, specific, current empirical support for each interpretive statement provides a very solid platform for psychologists in these settings.

Conclusion

In this chapter, I have presented material regarding the administration and scoring of the MMPI–2–RF, with a strong recommendation for the user to adopt computer-assisted administration and scoring. The next two chapters present the substantive interpretive guidelines. Chapter 3 focuses on the nine Protocol Validity Scales, and Chapter 4 presents interpretive guidelines for each of the 42 Substantive Scales, ordered by domain. Following that, Chapter 5 describes a clear, systematic interpretation strategy, and Chapter 6 presents a case example using this strategy.

Description and Interpretation of the Protocol Validity Scales

3

The inclusion of built-in measures of test-taking attitude has always been a hallmark feature of the Minnesota Multiphasic Personality Inventory (MMPI). For the first few decades, most users considered Cannot Say *(CNS)*, Lie *(L)*, Infrequency *(F)*, and Correction *(K)* to be the four indicators of protocol validity. Additional validity scales were developed over time, and the MMPI–2 included the significant additions of Variable Response Inconsistency *(VRIN)*, True Response Inconsistency *(TRIN)*, and Back F *(Fb)*, with Superlative Self-Presentation *(S)* added subsequently.

The MMPI–2—Restructured Form (MMPI–2–RF) now includes nine validity scales, each with a significant foundation of psychometric and validity research. Handel, Ben-Porath, Tellegen, and Archer (2010) provided convincing simulation data regarding the interpretation of Variable Response Inconsistency *(VRIN-r)* and True Response Inconsistency *(TRIN-r)*. Sellbom and Bagby (2008, 2010) presented data regarding overreporting and underreporting pathology on the MMPI–2–RF. Sellbom, Toomey, Wygant, Kucharski, and Duncan (2010) described a study on the detection of malingering. Ingram and Ternes (2016) recently published a meta-analysis on the overreporting scales.

---

http://dx.doi.org/10.1037/0000074-004
Assessment Using the MMPI–2–RF, by D. M. McCord

Understanding the test taker's attitude and approach toward the test is essential in the interpretation of the Substantive Scales. Thus, careful examination of the validity scales is always the first step. There are 10 indicators of validity, including one count and nine scales. These indicators are grouped into three categories of threat that reflect the overall conceptualization of protocol validity used in MMPI–2–RF interpretation. The first threat category addresses *content nonresponsiveness*, or the tendency of the test taker to give a response without basing it on an accurate reading or understanding of the item content. The second threat is *overreporting* of psychopathology, when the client is exaggerating his or her symptoms and level of dysfunction. The third threat is *underreporting* of psychopathology, when the client is minimizing or denying psychological dysfunction or problems.

Content Nonresponsiveness

As noted above, the content nonresponsiveness category of validity threat targets approaches to test taking that produce responses that are not based on item content. The importance here is that if the client is not responding based on an accurate reading or understanding of individual items, he or she cannot provide accurate and useful information related to the psychopathology constructs measured by the Substantive Scales of the MMPI–2–RF. There are three broad types of content nonresponsiveness: nonresponding, random responding, and fixed responding.

Nonresponding refers to the situation in which the test taker either skips an item entirely or endorses it as both true and false. In either case, the item is unscorable. An individual might omit an item for a wide range of reasons, including confusion, inability to read the specific item, cognitive deficiency related to understanding the content, test resistance or general oppositionality, or defensiveness. The impact of unscorable items is to artificially lower scores on Substantive Scales, risking underestimation of the level of dysfunction. Nonresponding is assessed with the *CNS* count.

Random responding involves an inconsistent, unsystematic pattern of responding to test items that is not based on an accurate reading or understanding of the content of the items. This pattern may be intentional or unintentional, and it can result from cognitive or reading deficiencies, confusion, or possibly lack of cooperation. Random responding is assessed with the *VRIN-r* scale.

Fixed responding is a consistent, systematic pattern of responding, but one that is not based on an accurate reading or understanding of the item content. This pattern consists of a tendency to answer *true* (i.e., acquiescence) or *false* (i.e., nonacquiescence) to most items, regardless of content. Fixed responding is assessed using the *TRIN-r* scale.

CANNOT SAY *(CNS)*

There are 338 items on the MMPI–2–RF, and *CNS* is simply the raw count of items that could not be scored. In most cases these are omitted items, but when using the paper-

and-pencil form of the test, it is possible for the client to answer both *true* and *false*, which also counts as unscorable and adds a point to *CNS*.

The impact of omitting an item is to lower the overall score for the scale on which the item occurs, which can lead to an underestimate of the true level of psychopathology. Empirical research has shown that if at least 90% of the items on a given scale are answered, the resulting score is still interpretable (Dragon, Ben-Porath, & Handel, 2012). Thus, in research protocols the standard is to exclude cases in which *CNS* ≥ 18; in clinical practice, when using the computer-generated scoring reports, it is recommended to apply the 90% standard on a scale-by-scale basis. Note that the percent of items completed is shown below each scale on the Score Report and bolded if < 90%. Text of omitted items is also included, along with a list of scales on which that item occurs. Table 3.1 provides interpretation guidelines for *CNS* scores.

VARIABLE RESPONSE INCONSISTENCY *(VRIN-r)*

The 53 item pairs in *VRIN-r* are similar in content, and thus the test taker's response should be the same, either true–true or false–false, for each pair. The raw score on *VRIN-r* is the total number of pairs in which responses differ, either true–false or false–true. The resulting *T* score is interpreted as reflecting random responding, which could be intentional, as when a test taker is not cooperating and possibly not even reading the items, or unintentional, which may be due to insufficient reading, cognitive, or language abilities. Note that high levels of random responding impact the interpretability of other Protocol Validity Scales as well as the Substantive Scales. It is important not to assume that elevated scores reflect intentional random responding by the test taker; other causes for inconsistent responding should be considered using collateral assessment data. Table 3.2 provides interpretation guidelines for *VRIN-r* scores.

TABLE 3.1

Interpretation of Cannot Say *(CNS)* Scores

Raw score	Validity issue	Possible reasons	Interpretive issues
≥15	Scores on some scales may be invalid.	Reading problems Severe psychopathology Obsessiveness Lack of cooperation Lack of insight	Examine content of omitted items for patterns. Check to see which specific scales are impacted. If < 90% of the items are scorable, the scale score may be invalid; in this case, the absence of scale elevation should not be interpreted as reflecting the absence of psychopathology.
1–14	Scores on some of the shorter scales may be invalid.	Specific, selected topics of nonresponsiveness	
0	None	Client responded to all 338 items.	Test taker was cooperative, at least with regard to responding to test items.

TABLE 3.2
Interpretation of Variable Response Inconsistency (*VRIN-r*) Scores

T score	Validity issue	Possible reasons	Interpretive issues
≥80	Protocol is invalid due to excessive variable response inconsistency.	Reading, language, or cognitive problems Intentional random responding Uncooperative approach to test taking	Protocol is uninterpretable.
70–79	There is some evidence of variable response inconsistency.	Reading, language, or cognitive problems Scoring errors Test taker carelessness	Scores on Protocol Validity and Substantive Scales should be interpreted with some caution.
39–69	There is evidence of consistent responding.	The test taker was able to understand and respond relevantly to the test items.	Protocol is interpretable.
30–38	There is evidence of remark-ably consistent responding.	The test taker was careful and deliberate in his or her approach to the assessment.	Protocol is interpretable.

TRUE RESPONSE INCONSISTENCY (*TRIN-r*)

The 26 item pairs in *TRIN-r* have content that is approximately reversed, and most individuals in the standardization sample answered the two items in opposite directions, that is, true–false or false–true. The raw score on *TRIN-r* is the number of pairs in which both items were answered *true* minus the number of pairs in which both items were marked false. This arithmetic adjustment means that high scores on *TRIN-r* indicate that the client tended to mark both items of a pair as *true* (an acquiescent response set), despite their reversed or opposite content, and low scores indicate that the client tended to mark both items as false (a nonacquiescent response set), despite their reversed content. Raw scores are converted to *T* scores, and *T* scores <50 are reflected to be the same distance >50 so that all Protocol Validity Scales work in the same direction, with high scores indicating invalid responding. *TRIN-r T* scores are marked with a T or F on the Score Report to indicate which response set (acquiescence or nonacquiescence) produced the elevation. Table 3.3 provides interpretation guidelines for *TRIN-r* scores.

Overreporting of Psychopathology

Overreporting occurs in many clinical settings and for a wide variety of reasons. In accurately understanding and describing clients' actual pattern of psychological dysfunction, it is essential to estimate the extent to which they might be reporting symptoms they do not really have or enhancing or exaggerating problems they do have on some level. Overreporting can be intentional or unintentional.

TABLE 3.3

Interpretation of True Response Inconsistency *(TRIN-r)* Scores

T score	Validity issue	Possible reasons	Interpretive issues
≥80T	Protocol is invalid due to excessive fixed, content-inconsistent true responding.	An uncooperative approach to test taking is likely.	Protocol is uninterpretable.
70–79T	There is some evidence of fixed, content-inconsistent true responding.	An uncooperative approach to test taking is likely.	Scores on Protocol Validity and Substantive Scales should be interpreted with some caution.
50–69	There is evidence of consistent responding.	Not applicable.	Protocol is interpretable.
70–79F	There is some evidence of fixed, content-inconsistent false responding.	An uncooperative approach to test taking is likely.	Scores on Protocol Validity and Substantive Scales should be interpreted with some caution.
≥80F	Protocol is invalid due to excessive fixed, content-inconsistent false responding.	An uncooperative approach to test taking is likely.	Protocol is uninterpretable.

Intentional overreporting occurs when test takers consciously select their responses to indicate higher levels of psychological dysfunction than they genuinely experience. This often occurs when the possibility exists for external gain (e.g., benefits, litigation settlements, attention). Overreporting does not necessarily reflect the absence of genuine psychopathology; it may just exaggerate the degree of psychological dysfunction that actually does exist.

Unintentional overreporting is also an approach that is exhibited by some clients. The process here is that the test takers are not aware that they are exaggerating symptoms and genuinely see themselves as experiencing the frequency and intensity of psychopathology they are endorsing. Diagnostic contexts in which unintentional overreporting might occur include somatoform disorders such as hypochondriasis and internalizing disorders that include catastrophizing.

The test-taking approach of overreporting has historically been recognized as a threat to the validity of self-report assessments and has had various labels, including *faking bad, feigning, negative response bias,* and *malingering. Overreporting* is a relatively value-free, descriptive term that is preferred by most current MMPI users. The MMPI–2–RF includes five overreporting scales: Infrequent Responses *(F-r),* Infrequent Psychopathology Responses *(Fp-r),* Infrequent Somatic Responses *(Fs),* Symptom Validity *(FBS),* and Response Bias *(RBS).*

INFREQUENT RESPONSES *(F-r)*

The 32 items of *F-r* are endorsed in the scored direction by fewer than 10% of the current normative sample. A significant empirical literature documents that elevated *F-r*

TABLE 3.4
Interpretation of Infrequent Responses *(F-r)* Scores

T score	Validity issue	Possible reasons	Interpretive issues
≥120	Protocol is invalid. Overreporting is reflected in an excessive number of infrequent responses.	Inconsistent responding Overreporting	Examine *VRIN-r* and *TRIN-r*. If inconsistency is ruled out, note that this level of overreporting is rare even in individuals with genuine, severe psychopathology. Substantive Scales cannot be interpreted.
100–119	Protocol may be invalid. Overreporting of psychological dysfunction is indicated by a considerably larger than average number of infrequent responses.	Inconsistent responding Severe psychopathology Severe emotional distress Overreporting	Inconsistency should be considered first. Examine *VRIN-r* and *TRIN-r*. If inconsistency is ruled out, genuine psychopathology is possible if evident in history or collateral data. Otherwise, overreporting is likely.
90–99	Possible overreporting of psychological dysfunction is indicated by a much larger than average number of infrequent responses.	Inconsistent responding Genuine, substantial psychopathology Significant emotional distress Overreporting	
79–89	Possible overreporting of psychological dysfunction is indicated by an above-average number of infrequent responses.	Inconsistent responding Significant psychopathology Significant emotional distress Overreporting	
<79	There is no evidence of overreporting.	Not applicable	Protocol is interpretable.

scores are associated with overreporting of a wide range of psychological, cognitive, and somatic symptoms. As *F-r* scores increases, more evidence of genuine psychopathology is needed in order to rule out overreporting. Table 3.4 provides interpretation guidelines for *F-r* scores.

INFREQUENT PSYCHOPATHOLOGY RESPONSES *(Fp-r)*

The 21 items of *Fp-r* were rarely answered (< 20%) by people with genuine, severe psychopathology, and there is no overlap with *F-r*. Some studies have shown that *Fp-r* is a more accurate measure of overreporting than *F-r*, especially in clinical populations, as scores are less confounded with actual psychopathology; however, other studies have shown that *F-r* is most accurate in many general populations. A general conclusion is that in clinical practice, it is useful to have multiple measures of overreporting. Table 3.5 provides interpretation guidelines for *Fp-r* scores.

INFREQUENT SOMATIC RESPONSES *(Fs)*

The 16 items of *Fs* were infrequently endorsed by medical patients known to have various physical diseases for which they were in treatment. Wygant, Ben-Porath, and Arbisi (2004) developed this scale for the purpose of assessing the overreporting of somatic symptoms. They first identified MMPI–2 items rarely endorsed by individuals in three very large archival samples of medical patients, and from the 166 items identified solely by frequency, they selected 16 with somatic content. Subsequent research has shown *Fs* to be specifically sensitive to the overreporting of somatic complaints. Table 3.6 provides interpretation guidelines for *Fs* scores.

TABLE 3.5

Interpretation of Infrequent Psychopathology Responses *(Fp-r)* Scores

T Score	Validity issue	Possible reasons	Interpretive issues
≥100	Protocol is invalid. Overreporting is reflected in a considerably larger than average number of responses rarely endorsed by individuals with genuine, severe psychopathology.	Inconsistent responding Overreporting	Examine *VRIN-r* and *TRIN-r*. If inconsistency is ruled out, note that this level of overreporting is rare even in individuals with genuine, severe psychopathology. Substantive Scales cannot be interpreted.
80–99	Possible overreporting of psychological dysfunction is indicated by a much larger than average number of responses rarely endorsed by individuals with genuine, severe psychopathology.	Inconsistent responding Severe psychopathology Overreporting	Examine *VRIN-r* and *TRIN-r*. Scores may reflect genuine, severe psychopathology, but exaggeration is possible. If there is no history or supporting evidence for psychopathology, overreporting is likely.
70–79	Possible overreporting of psychological dysfunction is indicated by an above-average number of responses rarely endorsed by individuals with genuine, severe psychopathology.	Inconsistent responding Severe psychopathology Overreporting	
<70	There is no evidence of overreporting.	Not applicable	Protocol is interpretable.

TABLE 3.6

Interpretation of Infrequent Somatic Responses *(Fs)* Scores

T score	Validity issue	Possible reasons	Interpretive issues
≥100	Scores on the Somatic/ Cognitive Scales may be invalid. Over-reporting is indicated by a very unusual combination of responses that is associated with noncredible reporting of somatic and/or cognitive symptoms.	Inconsistent responding Overreporting of somatic and/or cognitive symptoms	Examine *VRIN-r* and *TRIN-r*. If inconsistency is ruled out, note that the combination of responses is very rare even in individuals with substantial medical problems who report credible symptoms. Scores on somatic and/or cognitive scales should be interpreted with caution.
80–99	Possible overreporting is indicated by an unusual combination of responses that is associated with non-credible reporting of somatic and/or cognitive symptoms.	Inconsistent responding Significant and/ or multiple medical conditions Overreporting of somatic and/or cognitive complaints	Examine *VRIN-r* and *TRIN-r*. If inconsistency is ruled out, note that the combination of responses may occur in individuals with substantial medical problems who report credible symptoms, but it could also reflect exaggeration. Scores on somatic and/ or cognitive scales should be interpreted with caution.
<80	There is no evidence of overreporting.	Not applicable	Protocol is interpretable.

SYMPTOM VALIDITY *(FBS-r)*

The 30-item *FBS-r* is similar to *Fs* in that it is used to assess overreporting of somatic/ cognitive symptoms; it differs from *Fs* primarily in that it was developed in the context of civil litigation. There is extensive empirical research on this scale, and it is used frequently by forensic neuropsychologists. For *FBS-r* as well as *Fs*, extratest variables, especially those related to the context of the assessment, must be considered in order to make any inferences about possible reasons for overreporting. As suggested in the text boxes, elevated *Fs* or *FBS-r* scores limit the interpretability of the Somatic/Cognitive Scales. Table 3.7 provides interpretation guidelines for *FBS-r* scores.

RESPONSE BIAS SCALE *(RBS)*

The 28-item *RBS* was developed in the context of disability and personal injury claimants and is thus closely related to both *Fs* and *FBS-r*. Specifically, *RBS* was developed based on correlations with external, routinely used measures of symptom validity (the Test of Memory Malingering, the Word Memory Test, and the Computerized Assessment of Response Bias). Empirical research has demonstrated that

TABLE 3.7

Interpretation of Symptom Validity *(FBS-r)* Scores

T score	Validity issue	Possible reasons	Interpretive issues
≥100	Scores on the Somatic/Cognitive Scales may be invalid. Overreporting is indicated by a very unusual combination of responses that is associated with noncredible reporting of somatic and/or cognitive symptoms.	Inconsistent responding Overreporting of somatic and/or cognitive symptoms	Examine *VRIN-r* and *TRIN-r*. If inconsistency is ruled out, note that this combination of responses is very rare even in individuals with substantial medical problems who report credible symptoms. Scores on somatic and/or cognitive scales should be interpreted with caution.
80–99	Possible overreporting is indicated by an unusual combination of responses that is associated with noncredible reporting of somatic and/or cognitive symptoms.	Inconsistent responding Significant and/or multiple medical conditions Overreporting of somatic and/or cognitive complaints	Examine *VRIN-r* and *TRIN-r*. If inconsistency is ruled out, note that this combination of responses may occur in individuals with substantial medical problems who report credible symptoms, but it could also reflect exaggeration. Scores on somatic and/or cognitive scales should be interpreted with caution.
<80	There is no evidence of overreporting.	Not applicable	Protocol is interpretable.

RBS is particularly sensitive to the overreporting of memory problems. Table 3.8 provides interpretation guidelines for *RBS* scores.

Underreporting of Psychopathology

Underreporting is the term used when the test taker produces a self-report that describes a level of emotional and psychological functioning that is much better than would be suggested by a "true" objective assessment. In parallel with the preference of current MMPI users for the term *overreporting* rather than older, pejorative terms such as *faking bad, underreporting* is preferred to older terms such as *faking good* or the awkward *positive malingering*. The word *faking* clearly implies intentionality, an often-inaccurate inference avoided by the neutral terms of *overreporting* and *underreporting*. Underreporting is particularly common in certain predictable contexts, such as preemployment screening and custody determination evaluations, as well as in other situations in which it is advantageous to appear very well adjusted.

In cases of elevated scores, determining whether the underreporting is intentional or unintentional requires external corroborative data. If one or both of the

TABLE 3.8

Interpretation of Response Bias Scale *(RBS)* Scores

T score	Validity issue	Possible reasons	Interpretive issues
≥100	Scores on the Cognitive Complaints *(COG)* scale may be invalid. Overreporting is indicated by a very unusual combination of responses that is associated with noncredible memory complaints.	Inconsistent responding Overreporting of somatic and/or cognitive symptoms	Examine *VRIN-r* and *TRIN-r*. If inconsistency is ruled out, note that the combination of responses is very rare even in individuals with substantial emotional dysfunction who report credible symptoms. Scores on *COG* should be interpreted with caution.
80–99	Possible overreporting is indicated by an unusual combination of responses associated with noncredible memory complaints.	Inconsistent responding Significant emotional dysfunction Overreporting of memory complaints	Examine *VRIN-r* and *TRIN-r*. If inconsistency is ruled out, note that this combination of responses may occur in individuals with substantial emotional dysfunction who report credible symptoms, but it could also reflect exaggeration. Scores on *COG* should be interpreted with caution.
<80	There is no evidence of overreporting.	Not applicable	Protocol is interpretable.

underreporting scales—Uncommon Virtues *(L-r)* and Adjustment Validity *(K-r)*—are elevated and Substantive Scales are low, yet the case history reveals clear distress and turmoil, underreporting is very likely, and the protocol is thus likely to be unrepresentative of the individual. However, it is important to note that in some cases, *L-r* or *K-r* may be elevated for different reasons. Higher scores on *L-r* are sometimes found in rural, traditionally religious people, in whom high levels of virtuousness are expected, thus influencing self-perception. Higher scores on *K-r* may in fact reflect a high level of general psychological adjustment in an individual whose case history is consistent with that conclusion.

Finally, as was true with the overreporting scales, inconsistent responding can impact the measures of underreporting. In particular, because most items on *L-r* and *K-r* are scored when marked false, inconsistent fixed responding in the false direction can elevate these scales.

UNCOMMON VIRTUES *(L-r)*

The 14 items of *L-r* all describe minor faults, shortcomings, or imperfections to which most people are comfortable admitting. It is important in interpreting *L-r* to consider the possibility of a cultural or religious background that stresses virtuousness in self-perception. Table 3.9 provides interpretation guidelines for *L-r* scores.

TABLE 3.9

Interpretation of Uncommon Virtues *(L-r)* Scores

T score	Validity issue	Possible reasons	Interpretive issues
≥80	The protocol may be invalid. Underreporting is indicated by the test taker presenting himself or herself in an extremely positive light by denying minor faults and shortcomings that most people acknowledge.	Inconsistent responding Underreporting	Examine *VRIN-r* and *TRIN-r*. If inconsistency is ruled out, then note that this level of virtuous self-presentation is very uncommon even in individuals with backgrounds stressing traditional values. Any absence of elevation on the Substantive Scales is uninterpretable. Elevated scores on the Substantive Scales may underestimate the problems assessed by those scales.
70–79	Possible underreporting is indicated by the test taker presenting himself or herself in a very positive light by denying several minor faults and shortcomings that most people acknowledge.	Inconsistent responding Traditional upbringing Underreporting	If inconsistency is ruled out, then note that this level of virtuous self-presentation is uncommon but may reflect a background stressing traditional values. Any absence of elevation on the Substantive Scales should be interpreted with caution. Elevated scores on the Substantive Scales may underestimate the problems assessed by those scales.
65–69	Possible underreporting is indicated by the test taker presenting himself or herself in a positive light by denying some minor faults and shortcomings that most people acknowledge.	Inconsistent responding Traditional upbringing Underreporting	If inconsistency is ruled out, then note that this level of virtuous self-presentation may reflect a background stressing traditional values. Any absence of elevation on the Substantive Scales is uninterpretable. Elevated scores on the Substantive Scales may underestimate the problems assessed by those scales.
<65	There is no evidence of underreporting.	Not applicable	Protocol is interpretable.

ADJUSTMENT VALIDITY *(K-r)*

Elevated scores on the 14-item *K-r* suggest positive overall emotional and psychological adjustment. This is a dimensional construct, so higher scores reflect better adjustment. Although *K-r* is considered a measure of potential underreporting, it is also possible that the test taker is indeed well adjusted and is reporting accurately.

TABLE 3.10

Interpretation of Adjustment Validity (*K-r*) Scores

T score	Validity issue	Possible reasons	Interpretive issues
≥70	Underreporting is indicated by the test taker presenting himself or herself as remarkably well adjusted.	Inconsistent responding Underreporting	Examine *VRIN-r* and *TRIN-r*. If inconsistency is ruled out, then note that this level of psychological adjustment is rare in the general population. Any absence of elevation on the Substantive Scales should be interpreted with caution. Elevated scores on the Substantive Scales may underestimate the problems assessed by those scales.
66–69	Possible underreporting is reflected in the test taker presenting himself or herself as very well adjusted.	Inconsistent responding Very good psychological adjustment Underreporting	If inconsistency is ruled out, then note that this level of psychological adjustment is relatively rare in the general population. For individuals who are not exceptionally well adjusted, any absence of elevation on the Substantive Scales should be interpreted with caution. Elevated scores on the Substantive Scales may underestimate the problems assessed by those scales.
60–65	Possible underreporting is indicated by the test taker presenting himself or herself as well adjusted.	Inconsistent responding Good psychological adjustment Underreporting	If inconsistency is ruled out, then in individuals who are not well adjusted, any absence of elevation on the Substantive Scales should be interpreted with caution. Elevated scores on the Substantive Scales may underestimate the problems assessed by those scales.
<60	There is no evidence of underreporting.	Not applicable	Protocol is interpretable.

Contextual and other external data are essential in the interpretation of *K-r*. Table 3.10 provides interpretation guidelines for *K-r* scores.

Patterns of Protocol Validity Scale Scores

I have noted emphatically that in the interpretation of an MMPI–2–RF protocol, it is essential to first carefully consider the issue of protocol validity. The 10 validity indicators described in this chapter, and particularly the formal information provided in the tables, focus on the impact of response bias threats on the accuracy of the Substantive Scales. In this section, I briefly discuss the interrelationships among the validity indicators themselves—that is, the effects that Protocol Validity Scales have on each other.

As a reminder, the three main internal threats to protocol validity are content nonresponsiveness, overreporting, and underreporting. Content nonresponsiveness includes nonresponding (omitting or double-marking items), inconsistent random responding, inconsistent fixed true responding (acquiescence), and inconsistent fixed false responding (nonacquiescence). Content-based response biases include overreporting and underreporting. The interpretive material provided in the text boxes in this chapter contains frequent references to potential external threats to protocol validity as well. These threats include the presence of genuine, severe psychopathology; genuine medical conditions; rural, religious, or traditional background; and exceptionally positive adjustment. In the following sections I consider these threats, focusing primarily on the impact they might have on the other validity indicators.

NONRESPONDING

When a test taker omits items or double marks items, the effect is to lower the score below its theoretically "true" value on all other Protocol Validity and Substantive Scales. Thus, this indicator should always be the first one checked by the examiner. Ideally it should be checked immediately upon completion of the test, and if there are any omissions at all, the test taker should be encouraged to go back and complete the omitted items. Note that because omitting an item contributes to the scale score exactly as if the test taker had responded in the nonscored direction, the impact is always to lower the overall score. This applies not only to the Substantive Scales but to all nine of the Protocol Validity Scales as well; thus, the 90% rule should also apply when considering the validity scales. Generally, when fewer than 90% of the items have been answered, the examiner should consider the score on the validity scale in question to underestimate the true score and should modify interpretation accordingly.

Two specific situations require particular attention. First, four of the nine validity scales have specific cutoff scores that invalidate the profile: *VRIN-r* ≥ 80, *TRIN-r* ≥ 80, *F* = 120, and *Fp-r* ≥ 100. If the score is approaching these values and the percentage of responses is < 90, it is possible that the profile should be considered invalid based on the estimated true score. The second condition has to do with the shorter Substantive Scales of four or five items in which the omission of even a single item can render the scale uninterpretable. In summary, any time *CNS* > 0, the omitted items should be specifically examined for content and with regard to the scales on which they would have been scored.

INCONSISTENT RANDOM RESPONDING

Accurate responding to the MMPI–2–RF requires the test taker to read the item carefully, to be able to understand the meanings in the content of the item, and to respond honestly to that content. Random responding occurs when one more of these conditions are not met. When *VRIN-r* is in the range of 70 to 79, concerns are raised in this regard, and scores of 80 or higher render the protocol invalid based on inconsistent random responding.

It is essential to realize that random responding, as indicated by an elevated *VRIN-r* score, has the effect of artificially raising scores on all five of the overreporting scales and both underreporting scales. The first three overreporting scales (*F-r*, *Fp-r*, and *Fs*) are based on tabulating infrequent responses, so a random response set results in the endorsement of more scorable items on these three scales than would be produced in a valid, systematic approach; this is generally true for *FBS-r* and *RBS* as well. With regard to the underreporting scales *L-r* and *K-r*, both are composed of items scored primarily when marked false, so random responding artificially elevates these scales as well.

Random responding can in some cases reflect an intentionally uncooperative test taker, a hypothesis that should be evaluated in the context of other external and observational data. Unintentional random responding may, as noted above, reflect reading, comprehension, or cognitive limitations; these possibilities may be assessed with other appropriate assessment instruments or historical data. The practical implications of the distinctions here have to do with the advisability of retesting. If the client is being intentionally resistant, it may be possible to establish a more positive therapeutic relationship and to elicit a more cooperative approach to a second administration of the test. If the problem is purely a matter of basic reading skills, the auditory administration of the test may be considered. If cognitive problems, such as confusion or problems with attention and concentration, are temporary, it may be worthwhile to readminister the test at a later date.

INCONSISTENT FIXED (TRUE OR FALSE) RESPONDING

Although random responding can be unintentional or intentional, fixed responding is usually intentional. Fixed true responding is termed *acquiescence* and indicates that the test taker has endorsed the true option much of the time, whether or not it is responsive to the item content. Inconsistent fixed true responding has the effect of inflating scores on all five overreporting scales and suppressing scores on both of the underreporting scales. This is because either fixed response approach (true or false) results in endorsement of rarely occurring symptoms assessed by the overreporting scales, and most of the items on both *L-r* and *K-r* are scored in the false direction. Inconsistent fixed false responding artificially elevates scores on all five overreporting scales as well as both underreporting scales for the same reasons. As noted in the tables earlier in this chapter, scores ≥ 80 on either *VRIN-r* or *TRIN-r* render the protocol invalid, and scores < 70 indicate that the response pattern is sufficiently consistent to proceed with consideration of possible overreporting or underreporting.

OVERREPORTING

Overreporting occurs when the test taker endorses a level of psychological dysfunction that is notably greater than a theoretical "true" objective level. Overreporting may be intentional or unintentional, a distinction that is not inherently evident in the validity scale scores themselves and that must be assessed using external data. As noted above, the five measures of overreporting (*F-r*, *Fp-r*, *Fs*, *FBS-r*, and *RBS*) are artificially lowered by elevated *CNS* scores and artificially elevated by inconsistent responding (random or fixed). In turn, all five overreporting scales result in artificially raised scores on substantive measures of psychopathology; *Fs* and *FBS-r* also produce artificial elevations on reports of somatic problems.

Unintentional overreporting occurs when the scale score is higher than an objective "true" level of dysfunction but the test taker himself or herself believes the responses to be genuine and accurate. With the item content on the MMPI–2–RF, this unintentional overreporting can be focused on psychological dysfunction, such as depression, anxiety, or psychotic symptoms; cognitive dysfunction in attention, concentration, decision making, or memory; or somatic or medical complaints, such as pain or debilitation.

Genuine psychopathology can also elevate scores on these scales, particularly *F-r*; because this scale is most sensitive to psychopathology, the cut point for invalidation is set at 120, the highest score possible. Empirical research supports the conclusion that a score of 120 is rarely if ever achieved based solely on objective psychopathology and thus always indicates overreporting. As noted in the interpretation table for *F-r*, scores in the 100-to-119 range suggest that genuine, severe psychopathology is present but that overreporting should be evaluated using external data. Specifically, an *F-r* score in the 100-to-119 range might be accurate if the case history data show clear evidence of major psychological dysfunction; if such a history is absent, then overreporting becomes a more likely interpretation.

In summary, *F-r* is sensitive to overreporting of the broad array of issues in the test content, including psychopathology, cognitive problems, and somatic or medical problems. *Fp-r* is most sensitive to overreporting psychopathology specifically. *Fs* is most sensitive to overreporting medical or somatic complaints, *FBS-r* is most sensitive to overreporting cognitive complaints, and *RBS* is most sensitive to overreporting memory problems.

UNDERREPORTING

The underreporting response pattern suggests that the test taker is reporting a level of general psychological adjustment and functioning that is notably better than an objective assessment of the "true" level of adjustment and functioning. Underreporting can be either intentional or unintentional. Self-report measures of psychopathology are generally vulnerable to intentional underreporting, and this pattern is most problematic in certain situations in which positive functioning is clearly advantageous if not essential, such as preemployment assessments and child custody evaluations. In other cases, the test taker simply lacks good awareness of or insight into his or her psychological functioning, and underreporting of psychopathology is unintentional.

The two measures of underreporting, *L-r* and *K-r*, consist of items primarily scored when marked false (11 of the 14 for *L-r*, 12 of the 14 for *K-r*). Thus, scores can be artificially inflated by elevated inconsistent random responding as well as by inconsistent fixed false responding. They can be artificially suppressed by nonresponding and inconsistent fixed true responding. In addition, *L-r* can be elevated by certain religious, rural, or cultural traditions, and, very importantly, elevations on *K-r* can in some cases reflect genuinely positive adjustment rather than underreporting of psychopathology.

Description and Interpretation of the Substantive Scales

4

In this chapter I present interpretive information for the 42 Substantive Scales of the Minnesota Multiphasic Personality Inventory—2—Restructured Form (MMPI–2–RF). As noted in the closing section of Chapter 1, the approach promoted here is a two-pass strategy including a relatively brief overview of the protocol from a top-down hierarchical perspective, followed by a more systematic, thorough, scales-by-domain approach. The order of scale presentation in this chapter was chosen to support the second pass of the two, taking each of the content domains in turn, and then going from broad to narrow within that domain. I refer the reader again to Figure 1.1, the hierarchical–dimensional assessment model reflected by the MMPI–2–RF Substantive Scales; in this chapter I will be moving from left to right across the domains, then top to bottom within each domain. In this approach I am also following the MMPI–2–RF Interpretation Worksheet, an important tool that will be presented in the next chapter. The expectation is that the reader will actively refer to this chapter as the Interpretation Worksheet is completed, a task facilitated by having the scales ordered in parallel.

As in Chapter 3, each of the scales is presented with a descriptive paragraph and then a text box with formal interpretive statements suggested for

---

The text boxes in this chapter were adapted from *Interpreting the MMPI–2–RF*, by Yossef S. Ben-Porath. Copyright © 2012 by the Regents of the University of Minnesota. Reproduced by permission of the University of Minnesota Press. All rights reserved.

http://dx.doi.org/10.1037/0000074-005
Assessment Using the MMPI–2–RF, by D. M. McCord

report writing. These text boxes are designed for practical reference as the clinician is preparing a report, and they have three sections. The first includes statements reflecting content-based interpretation of the scale based on *T* score; thus, it is quite appropriate to introduce these statements with language like, "The patient/client reports that . . ." The second section presents empirically established correlates for the scale; these may be appropriately included with a qualifier such as, "Other patients/clients with similar elevations are described as . . ." Finally, the third section includes suggestions, largely from the test authors, regarding diagnostic issues and treatment recommendations to consider.

Somatic/Cognitive Scales

There are six scales in the Somatic/Cognitive domain. The broadest is Somatic Complaints *(RC1)*, followed by five Specific Problems Scales: Malaise *(MLS)*, Gastrointestinal Complaints *(GIC)*, Head Pain Complaints *(HPC)*, Neurological Complaints *(NUC)*, and Cognitive Complaints *(COG)*. This important set of scales addresses a range of physical, somatic complaints. From an integrated care perspective, this is an essential domain to assess, and it is in some ways a bridge between the Protocol Validity Scales measuring the client's approach to test taking and the Substantive Scales in the other major domains. The physical health care professional is interested in knowing to what extent psychological factors may be contributing to the patient's presentation; conversely, the behavioral health care professional is interested in potential physical issues that may be contributing to the emotional, behavioral, and social issues presented. In interpreting these six scales, it is important to consider elevations on three particular Protocol Validity Scales: Infrequent Somatic Responses *(Fs)*, Symptom Validity *(FBS-r)*, and Response Bias *(RBS)*.

From the perspective that the MMPI–2–RF model of psychopathology consists of hierarchically arranged dimensional constructs ranging in scope from relatively broad to relatively narrow, note that the ordering of scales here in part reflects breadth. Although there is no Higher-Order Scale for this domain, *RC1* itself is a lengthy, broad scale spanning a wide range of physical complaints. *MLS*, though technically a Specific Problems Scale with just eight items, is the next-broadest in concept. Three very specific symptom scales—*GIC, HPC,* and *NUC*—follow that. Finally, *COG* is presented. This scale is somewhat broader in that it covers issues like memory, concentration, decision making, and intellectual limitations. It was initially grouped with the Internalizing Scales but was ultimately moved to the Somatic/Cognitive domain, intentionally placed next to the Emotional/Internalizing Dysfunction *(EID)* scale.

SOMATIC COMPLAINTS *(RC1)*

The content of the 27 items on *RC1* includes a wide range of physical symptoms and complaints. Moderate elevations may reflect the presence of genuine physical health problems, and these should be carefully considered. As the elevation increases, so does the likelihood that psychological factors are playing a role in the presentation. That is, the wide range of somatic symptoms included in the item content suggests that higher elevations are produced by a combination of many types of symptoms that infrequently co-occur. It is always important to ensure that a medical evaluation of the complaints has been, or will be, conducted.

Interpretation Guidelines for Somatic Complaints *(RC1)* Scores

Content-based interpretation:

$T < 39$	Client reports a sense of physical well-being.
$T = 65–79$	Client reports multiple physical complaints that may include gastrointestinal, head pain, and neurological symptoms.
$T \geq 80$	Client reports a diffuse pattern of physical complaints that span multiple bodily symptoms.

Empirically, other individuals with elevations on this scale

- are focused on health-related concerns
- tend to develop physical symptoms in response to stress
- complain of tiredness and general fatigue
- may have a psychological component to their somatic complaints

Additional diagnostic and treatment considerations:

- The presence of a conversion disorder should be considered if Shyness *(SHY)* score is ≤ 39 and Cynicism *(RC3)* score is ≤ 39.
- Individuals with elevated *RC1* tend to be resistant to psychological interpretations of their somatic complaints.

MALAISE *(MLS)*

MLS, with eight items, describes a broad, general sense of poor health and physical debilitation, whereas *GIC, HPC*, and *NUC* describe specific types of somatic symptoms that are being reported. If none of these is elevated, *MLS* likely reflects a vague, nonspecific sense of poor health and fatigue. Elevated *MLS* scores are correlated with a preoccupation with health problems, sleep problems, and reported depression. Consider elevations on validity scales *Fs* and *FBS-r* when interpreting this scale.

Interpretation Guidelines for Malaise *(MLS)* Scores

Content-based interpretation:

$T < 39$	Client reports a generalized sense of physical well-being.
$T = 65–79$	Client reports experiencing poor health and feeling weak or tired.
$T \geq 80$	Client reports a general sense of malaise manifested in poor health and feeling tired, weak, and incapacitated.

Empirically, other individuals with elevations on this scale

- are preoccupied with poor health
- are likely to complain of
  - sleep disturbance
  - fatigue
  - low energy
  - sexual dysfunction

Additional diagnostic and treatment considerations:

- If a physical origin of symptoms has been ruled out, somatoform disorder is possible.
- Malaise may interfere with the client's willingness or ability to engage in treatment.

GASTROINTESTINAL COMPLAINTS *(GIC)*

The content of the five items on *GIC* covers a variety of gastrointestinal problems, including nausea, vomiting, upset stomach, and poor appetite. Gastrointestinal complaints are one of the most common categories of complaints in primary medical care settings, and medical evaluation of these symptoms is important. If a physical cause has been ruled out, it is possible that symptoms are stress related. As is the case with all scales in the Somatic/Cognitive domain, it is important to consider elevations on *Fs* when interpreting *GIC*. The test authors caution, however, that elevated *Fs* scores do not automatically invalidate the profile, nor do they indicate that the test taker is intentionally overreporting somatic symptoms. One recommendation is that if *Fs* ≥ 100 and *GIC* is elevated, the clinician should use content-based interpretive statements but avoid other empirical correlates.

Interpretation Guidelines for Gastrointestinal Complaints *(GIC)* Scores

Content-based interpretation:

T = 65–89	Client reports a number of gastrointestinal complaints.
T ≥ 90	Client reports a large number of gastrointestinal complaints such as poor appetite, nausea, vomiting, and recurrent upset stomach.

Empirically, other individuals with elevations on this scale

- have a history of gastrointestinal problems
- are preoccupied with health concerns

Additional diagnostic and treatment considerations:

- If a physical origin of gastrointestinal problems has been evaluated and ruled out, somatoform disorder should be considered.
- Stress-reduction intervention should be considered.

HEAD PAIN COMPLAINTS *(HPC)*

HPC includes six items describing various complaints about head and neck pain. Elevated scores are associated with these specific concerns as well as a more general preoccupation with pain-related issues and with other more diffuse somatic complaints. As is true for all scales in the Somatic/Cognitive domain, it is important to obtain medical evaluation of these complaints. It is also essential to consider elevations on *Fs*. If *Fs* ≥ 100 and *HPC* is elevated, the clinician should use content-based interpretive statements but avoid other empirical correlates.

Interpretation Guidelines for Head Pain Complaints *(HPC)* Scores

Content-based interpretation:

T = 65–79	Client reports head pain.
T ≥ 80	Client reports diffuse head and neck pain, recurring headaches, and development of head pain when upset.

Empirically, other individuals with elevations on this scale

- present with multiple somatic complaints
- are prone to develop physical symptoms in response to stress
- are preoccupied with physical health problems
- tend to complain about
  - headaches
  - chronic pain
  - difficulty concentrating

Additional diagnostic and treatment considerations:

- If a physical origin of head pain complaints has been evaluated and ruled out, somatoform disorder should be considered.
- Pain management techniques should be considered.

NEUROLOGICAL COMPLAINTS *(NUC)*

The content of the 10-item *NUC* scale describes various problems that are suggestive of a neurological origin, including weakness, numbness, dizziness, and involuntary movements. Again, interpreting elevations on this scale must be done in the context of medical, neurological, or neuropsychological evaluation. As with other scales in this domain, in interpreting *NUC* it is important to consider elevations on *Fs* in terms of overreporting of general somatic symptoms, *FBS-r* in terms of overreporting of cognitive symptoms, and *RBS* in terms of overreporting of memory symptoms.

Interpretation Guidelines for Neurological Complaints *(NUC)* Scores

Content-based interpretation:

$T = 65–91$	Client reports vague neurological complaints.
$T \geq 92$	Client reports a large number of various neurological complaints (e.g., dizziness, loss of balance, numbness, weakness, paralysis, loss of control over movement including involuntary movements).

Empirically, other individuals with elevations on this scale

- present with multiple somatic complaints
- are prone to develop physical symptoms in response to stress
- are likely to present with
  - dizziness
  - coordination difficulties
  - sensory problems

Additional diagnostic and treatment considerations:

- If a physical origin of neurological complaints has been evaluated and ruled out, somatoform disorder should be considered. (Conversion disorder should be considered if Shyness *(SHY)* score is ≤ 39 and Cynicism *(RC3)* score is ≤ 39.)
- Pain management techniques should be considered.

COGNITIVE COMPLAINTS *(COG)*

The 10 items of *COG* describe various cognitive difficulties, particularly problems with concentration, confusion, and memory and general intellectual limitations. Elevations on this scale are associated with poor stress tolerance and poor frustration tolerance. Recall from Chapter 3 that elevations on *FBS-r* suggest noncredible reporting of cognitive symptoms; thus, elevations on *COG* must be interpreted only in the context of scores on *FBS-r* (and possibly *RBS* specifically with regard to memory). One empirical study (Gervais, Ben-Porath, & Wygant, 2009) indicated that elevated *COG* scores are associated with subjective complaints of both emotional and cognitive problems but not with actual cognitive deficits. This distinction is important and points to the importance of having actual cognitive performance data as well as Protocol Validity Scales results when fully interpreting the meaning of an elevation on *COG*.

Interpretation Guidelines for Cognitive Complaints *(COG)* Scores

Content-based interpretation:

$T = 65–80$	Client reports a diffuse pattern of cognitive difficulties.
$T \geq 81$	Client reports a pattern of cognitive difficulties including memory problems, difficulties concentrating, intellectual limitations, and confusion.

Empirically, other individuals with elevations on this scale

- complain about memory problems
- have a low tolerance for frustration
- experience difficulties in concentration

Additional diagnostic and treatment considerations:

- The origin of cognitive complaints, which may require a neuropsychological evaluation, should be determined.

Internalizing Scales

The Internalizing domain is the broadest and most fully elaborated domain in the MMPI–2–RF assessment model (refer again to Figure 1.1). Of the 40 psychopathology constructs included in this hierarchical model, 15 are in the Internalizing domain. With constructs at all three primary levels of breadth (higher-order, midlevel, and narrow), this domain is a relatively elaborate hierarchical structure in itself. One of the three Higher-Order Scales, Emotional/Internalizing Dysfunction *(EID)*, is at the top of this structure. Three Restructured Clinical (RC) Scales form the intermediate level: Demoralization *(RCd)*, Low Positive Emotions *(RC2)*, and Dysfunctional Negative Emotions *(RC7)*.

Recent research on internalizing dysfunction has suggested a three-factor structure, including Demoralization/Distress, Depressivity/Anhedonia, and Anxiety/Fear (see Sellbom, Ben-Porath, & Bagby, 2008). *RCd*, *RC2*, and *RC7*, respectively, serve as markers for these factors, providing a linkage between the MMPI–2–RF assessment model and current theoretical models of internalizing dysfunction.

Finally, more specific scales provide facet-level information within each of the three strands represented by the RC Scales. Under *RCd* are Suicidal/Death Ideation *(SUI)*, Helplessness/Hopelessness *(HLP)*, Self-Doubt *(SFD)*, and Inefficacy *(NFC)*. Under *RC2* is Introversion/Low Positive Emotionality–Revised *(INTR-r)*. Under *RC7* are Stress/Worry *(STW)*, Anxiety *(AXY)*, Anger Proneness *(ANP)*, Behavior-Restricting Fears *(BRF)*, Multiple Specific Fears *(MSF)*, and Negative Emotionality/Neuroticism–Revised *(NEGE-r)*. These 15 scales are presented in the order that reflects the interpretive approach described in Chapter 5, which also parallels the Interpretive Worksheet. That is, I start with the Higher-Order *EID* scale, followed by *RCd* (and its four facet scales), *RC2* (and its single facet scale), and *RC7* (and its six facet scales).

EMOTIONAL/INTERNALIZING DYSFUNCTION *(EID)*

The content of the 41 items in *EID* span a broad range of emotional and internalizing problems, and most items also occur on one of the three midlevel scales, *RCd*, *RC2*, or *RC7*. Content domains include sadness, hopelessness, feelings of worthlessness, depression, lack of positive emotional experiences, fear, stress, and anxiety. Thus, this Higher-Order scale score may be interpreted as an overall indicator of the client's emotional functioning. Low scores can be interpreted as a below-average level of emotional difficulties, whereas high scores indicate that the client has endorsed a wide range of internalizing and emotional problems. The precise nature of these problems is reflected in the midlevel and specific-level constructs within this domain.

Interpretation Guidelines for Emotional/Internalizing Dysfunction *(EID)* Scores

Content-based interpretation:

$T < 39$	Client reports better-than-average level of emotional adjustment.
$T = 65–79$	Client's responses indicate significant emotional distress.
$T \geq 80$	Client's responses indicate considerable emotional distress that is likely to be perceived as a crisis.

Empirically, other individuals with elevations on this scale

- endorse a broad range of symptoms and difficulties associated with demoralization, low positive emotions, and negative emotional experiences (e.g., low morale, depression, anxiety; feelings of being overwhelmed, helpless, pessimistic)

Additional diagnostic and treatment considerations:

- The presence of internalizing disorders should be evaluated.
- Emotional distress may motivate the client to engage in treatment.

DEMORALIZATION *(RCd)*

RCd, with 24 items, is a very important broad scale that reflects a core concept that guided the restructuring of the MMPI–2. This scale directly assesses *demoralization*, which the test authors define as "a pervasive and affect-laden dimension of unhappiness and life satisfaction" (Ben-Porath & Tellegen, 2008/2011). Recall from Chapter 1 that this was the common factor that pervaded the MMPI and MMPI–2 and was present to varying degrees in all eight of the Clinical Scales. Now isolated and measured separately, Demoralization/Distress is the first factor of the three-factor conceptualization of internalizing dysfunction presented earlier in this section.

Interpretation Guidelines for Demoralization *(RCd)* Scores

Content-based interpretation:

$T < 39$	Client reports a higher-than-average level of morale and life satisfaction.
$T = 65–79$	Client reports being sad and unhappy and being dissatisfied with his or her current life circumstances.
$T \geq 80$	Client's responses indicate he or she is experiencing considerable emotional turmoil, is feeling overwhelmed, and is extremely unhappy, sad, and dissatisfied with his or her life.

Empirically, other individuals with elevations on this scale

- are at risk for suicidal ideation (if Suicidal/Death Ideation *[SUI]* or Helplessness/Hopelessness *[HLP]* scores are > 65)
- complain about depression or anxiety
- feel pessimistic and hopeless about the future
- have low self-esteem
- feel incapable of dealing with current life circumstances
- have difficulty concentrating
- are worry prone and ruminative
- feel sad, pessimistic, and/or insecure

Additional diagnostic and treatment considerations:

- The presence of a depression-related disorder should be evaluated.
- The presence of self-harm should be evaluated.
- Emotional distress may motivate the client to engage in treatment.
- Relief of psychological distress should be an initial target for intervention.

SUICIDAL/DEATH IDEATION *(SUI)*

The five-item *SUI* directly assesses suicidal thoughts, intention, and attempts and any history of these. Empirical research in recent years has been strongly supportive of the validity and practical usefulness of this scale (e.g., Glassmire, Tarescavage, Burchett, Martinez, & Gomez, 2016). The scale is unique in that endorsing even one of the five items results in a clinical-range *T* score. This scale is also one of the seven scales identified by the authors as having critical content; thus, it is highlighted in the computer-generated Score Reports, and any items endorsed in the scored direction are printed out in full. As discussed in Chapter 2, if at all possible the MMPI–2–RF should be scored while the client is still present so that at least a brief follow-up interview can clarify any item-level responses. Clearly, the clinician would note elevation on the *SUI* scale and query each endorsed item in the context of a suicide assessment.

Interpretation Guidelines for Suicidal/Death Ideation *(SUI)* Scores

Content-based interpretation:

T = 65–99 Client reports a history of suicidal ideation and/or attempts.
T = 100 Client reports current suicidal ideation and a history of suicidal ideation and attempts.

Empirically, other individuals with elevations on this scale

- are preoccupied with suicide and death
- are at risk for suicide attempt (risk is exacerbated by poor impulse control if Behavioral/Externalizing Dysfunction *[BXD]*, Antisocial Behavior *[RC4]*, Hypomanic Activation *[RC9]*, or Disconstraint–Revised *[DISC-r]* scores are ≥ 65 and/or by substance use if Substance Abuse *[SUB]* score is ≥ 65)
- may have recently attempted suicide
- may experience helplessness and hopelessness

Additional diagnostic and treatment considerations:

- Risk for suicide should be assessed immediately.

HELPLESSNESS/HOPELESSNESS *(HLP)*

The five items on *HLP* describe beliefs that the individual is incapable of overcoming his or her problems and of making the changes necessary to reach his or her life goals. Elevated scores reflect the feeling that life is a strain as well as feelings of being hopeless and helpless, being overwhelmed, believing that one got a raw deal from life, and lacking motivation for change. Feelings of hopelessness have been identified as relevant in the assessment of suicide risk and of nonsuicidal self-injury. Negative expectations regarding the future are associated with risk for depressive and anxiety disorders. As with *SUI*, *HLP* has been designated one of the seven scales having critical content. Thus, the Score Report highlights this scale and includes the full text of all items answered in the scored direction.

Interpretation Guidelines for Helplessness/Hopelessness *(HLP)* Scores

Content-based interpretation:

T = 65–79 Client reports feeling hopeless and pessimistic.
T ≥ 80 Client reports believing he or she cannot change and overcome his or her problems and is thus incapable of reaching his or her life goals.

Empirically, other individuals with elevations on this scale

- feel hopeless and pessimistic
- feel overwhelmed and that life is a strain
- believe they cannot be helped
- believe they got a raw deal from life
- lack motivation for change

Additional diagnostic and treatment considerations:

- Early targets for intervention should be loss of hope and feelings of despair.

SELF-DOUBT *(SFD)*

The four-item *SFD* scale describes a lack of confidence and a feeling of being useless. Elevated scores indicate feelings of insecurity as well as inferiority in comparison with others. Although this concept is closely related to the next scale, Inefficacy *(NFC)*, there are important differences as well. Low self-esteem has been suggested as a precursor to depression, and self-doubt is a risk factor for suicidal ideation, over and above effects accounted for by depression itself. Self-doubt has also been associated with borderline and avoidant personality patterns, eating disorders, and posttraumatic stress disorder. Self-esteem issues can be good targets for therapy.

Interpretation Guidelines for Self-Doubt *(SFD)* Scores

Content-based interpretation:

$T = 65$–69	Client reports feelings of self-doubt.
$T \geq 70$	Client reports feeling useless and lacking confidence.

Empirically, other individuals with elevations on this scale

- feel inferior and insecure
- are self-disparaging
- are prone to rumination
- are intropunitive
- present with lack of confidence and feelings of uselessness

Additional diagnostic and treatment considerations:

- Early targets for intervention should be low self-esteem and self-doubt.

INEFFICACY *(NFC)*

The content of the nine items on *NFC* assesses the extent to which the test taker feels incapable of making decisions and unable to deal effectively with even minor life crises. Low scores are interpreted as reflecting a sense of personal control and self-reliance. Elevated scores suggest that the test taker is likely to be passive and lacking in self-reliance when faced with difficulties. The empirical research related to this construct is based on part on Bandura's (1977) concept of self-efficacy; though Bandura himself stressed that this important human characteristic is domain specific, research has supported the idea of a generalized form of self-efficacy, and this is the primary concept measured by *NFC* (see, e.g., Judge, Erez, Bono, & Thoresen, 2002).

Interpretation Guidelines for Inefficacy *(NFC)* Scores

Content-based interpretation:

$T < 39$	Client did not endorse items on indecisiveness and ineffectualness.
$T = 65$–79	Client reports being passive, indecisive, and inefficacious and believing he or she is incapable of coping with current difficulties.

$T \geq 80$	Client reports being very indecisive and inefficacious, believing he or she is incapable of making decisions and dealing effectively with crises, and/or having difficulties dealing with small, inconsequential matters.

Empirically, other individuals with abnormally high or low scores on this scale (as noted)

- are likely to be self-reliant and power-oriented (if $T < 39$)
- are unlikely to be self-reliant and are likely passive (if $T \geq 65$)

Additional diagnostic and treatment considerations:

- Indecisiveness may interfere with establishing treatment goals and progress in treatment.

LOW POSITIVE EMOTIONS *(RC2)*

The 17-item *RC2* marks the second factor, Depressivity/Anhedonia, of the three-factor conceptualization of internalizing dysfunction described earlier in this chapter. As a relatively focused measure of anhedonia, *RC2* is of essential importance when evaluating depression-related dysfunction. From a neurobiological perspective, *RC2* (anhedonia) is more connected to reward pathways than to fear–threat pathways. Thus, it is also more strongly associated with serotonin deficiency, which has direct implications for treatment. Many patients present with a verbal self-description of depression; for many, Demoralization *(RCd)* may be significantly elevated, but this result may be more reflective of distress than of anhedonia. *RC2* is increasingly seen as a distinct indicator of major depression.

Interpretation Guidelines for Low Positive Emotions *(RC2)* Scores

Content-based interpretation:

$T < 39$	Client reports a high level of psychological well-being, a wide range of emotionally positive experiences, and feelings of confidence and energy.
$T \geq 65$	Client reports a lack of positive emotional experiences, significant anhedonia, and a lack of interest.

Empirically, other individuals with abnormally high or low scores on this scale (as noted)

- are optimistic, extroverted, and socially engaged (if $T < 39$)
- are pessimistic, socially introverted, socially disengaged, and lacking in energy and may display vegetative symptoms of depression (if $T \geq 65$)

Additional diagnostic and treatment considerations:

- The presence of depression-related disorder, including major depression (if $T \geq 75$), should be evaluated.
- The need for antidepressant medication should be evaluated, and inpatient treatment for major depression may be warranted (if $T \geq 75$).
- Anhedonia is a target for intervention.
- Low positive emotionality may interfere with engagement in treatment.

INTROVERSION/LOW POSITIVE EMOTIONALITY–REVISED *(INTR-r)*

INTR-r, with 20 items, is one of the Personality Psychopathology Five (PSY–5) Scales. Although not the exact equivalent of a facet of *RC2*, as it, too, is theoretically broad in scope, in this interpretive framework *INTR-r* is treated as a corroborative measure of low positive emotions. *INTR-r* is a scale with content reflecting low positive emotional experiences as well as social disengagement and avoidance of social situations and interactions. Low scores are readily interpretable and suggest that the test taker is extroverted and inclined to be socially active and to experience wide range of emotionally positive experiences. Elevated scores are indicative of social introversion, anhedonia, restricted interested, and a pessimistic outlook.

Interpretation Guidelines for Introversion/Low Positive Emotionality–Revised *(INTR-r)* Scores

Content-based interpretation:

$T < 39$	Client reports feeling energetic and having many emotionally positive experiences.
$T \geq 65$	Client reports a lack of positive emotional experiences and a tendency to avoid social situations.

Empirically, other individuals with elevations on this scale

- lack positive emotional experiences
- experience significant problems with anhedonia
- complain about depression
- lack interests
- are pessimistic
- are socially introverted

Additional diagnostic and treatment considerations:

- The need for antidepressant medication should be evaluated.
- Lack of positive emotions may interfere with engagement in therapy.

DYSFUNCTIONAL NEGATIVE EMOTIONS *(RC7)*

RC7, with 24 items, marks the third factor, Anxiety/Fear, of the three-factor conceptualization of internalizing dysfunction described earlier. It is designed to measure the test taker's reports of a variety of negative emotional experiences, including anxiety, fear, and anger. Low scores can be interpreted as indicative of below-average levels of reported negative emotional experiences. High scores are associated with an increased risk of anxiety-related psychopathology.

Interpretation Guidelines for Dysfunctional Negative Emotions *(RC7)* Scores

Content-based interpretation:

$T < 39$	Client reports a below-average level of negative emotional experience.
$T \geq 65$	Client reports various negative emotional experiences, including anxiety, anger, and fear.

Empirically, other individuals with elevations on this scale

- are inhibited behaviorally because of negative emotions
- experience intrusive ideation
- are anger prone
- are stress reactive
- experience problems with sleep, including nightmares
- worry excessively
- engage in excessive rumination
- perceive others as overly critical
- are self-critical and guilt prone

Additional diagnostic and treatment considerations:

- The presence of anxiety-related disorders should be evaluated.
- Emotional discomfort may motivate the client for treatment.
- Dysfunctional negative emotions are targets of intervention.
- The need for antianxiety medication should be considered (if $T \geq 80$).

STRESS/WORRY *(STW)*

The seven items of *STW* assess experiences of stress and worry, including preoccupation with disappointments, problems with time pressure, and specific worries about finances and misfortune. The broader concept of excessive worry is a key trait of generalized anxiety. Low scores can be interpreted as reflecting a below-average level of stress and worry. Elevated scores are associated with being stress reactive and worry prone and engaging in excessive rumination.

Interpretation Guidelines for Stress/Worry *(STW)* Scores

Content-based interpretation:

$T < 39$	Client reports a below-average level of stress and worry.
$T = 65–79$	Client reports an above-average level of stress and worry.
$T \geq 80$	Client reports multiple problems involving experiences of stress and worry, including preoccupation with disappointments, difficulties with time pressure, and specific worries about misfortune and finances.

Empirically, other individuals with elevations on this scale

- are stress reactive
- are worry prone
- engage in excessive rumination

Additional diagnostic and treatment considerations:

- The presence of stress-related disorders and for obsessive–compulsive disorder should be evaluated.
- Excessive worry and rumination are appropriate targets for intervention.
- Stress management techniques should be considered.

ANXIETY *(AXY)*

The five items of *AXY* focus specifically on experiences indicative of anxiety. Items describe frequent experiences of pervasive anxiety, fright, and nightmares. Elevated scores are correlated with significant anxiety and associated problems, including intrusive ideation, sleep difficulties, and posttraumatic distress. If the case history includes documentation of trauma, elevated *AXY* may indicate posttraumatic stress disorder. Because these items were rarely endorsed in the normative sample, a raw score of only 2 produces a *T* score in the clinical range. *AXY* is one of the seven scales with critical item content; thus, the Score Report will include full text of all items endorsed in the scored direction.

Interpretation Guidelines for Anxiety *(AXY)* Scores

Content-based interpretation:

T = 65–99	Client reports feeling anxious.
T = 100	Client reports feeling constantly anxious, often feeling that something dreadful is about to happen, being frightened by something every day, and having frequent nightmares.

Empirically, other individuals with elevations on this scale

- experience significant anxiety and anxiety-related problems
- experience intrusive ideation
- have sleep difficulties, including nightmares
- experience posttraumatic stress

Additional diagnostic and treatment considerations:

- The presence of anxiety-related disorders, including posttraumatic stress disorder, should be evaluated.
- The need for antianxiety medication should be considered (if $T \geq 80$).

ANGER PRONENESS *(ANP)*

The seven items of *ANP* describe anger and anger-related issues, including being impatient, getting upset easily, and becoming angered easily. Elevations on *ANP* are associated with temper tantrums, grudges, and other anger management problems. This construct is distinct from aggression and specifically addresses the negative emotionality component and the expression of anger rather than actual aggressive actions (see, for comparison, Aggression *[AGG]* and Aggressiveness–Revised *[AGGR-r]* within the Externalizing domain). It is also distinct from hostility, which is best measured by Cynicism *(RC3)*.

Interpretation Guidelines for Anger Proneness *(ANP)* Scores

Content-based interpretation:

T = 65–79	Client reports being anger prone.
T = 80	Client reports getting upset easily, being impatient with others, becoming easily angered, and being sometimes overcome by anger.

Empirically, other individuals with elevations on this scale

- have problems with anger, irritability, and low tolerance for frustration
- hold grudges
- have temper tantrums
- are argumentative

Additional diagnostic and treatment considerations:

- The presence of anger-related disorders should be evaluated.
- Anger management treatment should be considered.

BEHAVIOR-RESTRICTING FEARS *(BRF)*

The nine items of *BRF* have content describing fears that significantly restrict normal activities both in and outside of the home. *BRF* is associated with agoraphobia and more generally with fearfulness. *BRF* and the next scale, Multiple Specific Fears *(MSF)*, represent the distinction made in the *Diagnostic and Statistical Manual of Mental Disorders* (American Psychiatric Association, 2013) between agoraphobic dysfunction and simple phobias. An elevated score on *BRF* suggests that behavior-restricting fears are likely to be appropriate targets for therapeutic intervention.

Interpretation Guidelines for Behavior-Restricting Fears *(BRF)* Scores

Content-based interpretation:

$T = 65–89$	Client reports multiple fears that significantly restrict normal activity in and outside the home.
$T \geq 90$	Client reports multiple fears that significantly restrict normal activity in and outside the home, including fears of leaving home, open spaces, small spaces, the dark, sharp objects, and handling money.

Empirically, other individuals with elevations on this scale

- display agoraphobia
- are fearful

Additional diagnostic and treatment considerations:

- The presence of anxiety disorders, particularly agoraphobia, should be evaluated.
- Behavior-restricting fears should be considered as targets for intervention.

MULTIPLE SPECIFIC FEARS *(MSF)*

The nine items of *MSF* reflect anxiety-producing fears of specific objects or situations, with content including animals, acts of nature, blood, injection, injury, and other issues. Individuals who produce elevated *MSF* scores tend to be risk averse and harm avoidant, and they are at increased risk for specific phobias.

Interpretation Guidelines for Multiple Specific Fears *(MSF)* Scores

Content-based interpretation:

$T < 39$	Client reports a lower-than-average number of specific fears.
$T = 65–77$	Client reports multiple specific fears of certain animals and acts of nature.
$T = 78$	Client reports multiple specific fears such as blood, fire, thunder, water, natural disasters, spiders, mice, and other animals.

Empirically, other individuals with elevations on this scale

- are risk averse
- are harm avoidant

Additional diagnostic and treatment considerations:

- The presence of specific phobias should be evaluated.
- Specific fears can be targets for intervention.

NEGATIVE EMOTIONALITY/ NEUROTICISM–REVISED *(NEGE-r)*

NEGE-r is a 20-item PSY–5 scale that corresponds to the Neuroticism domain of the five-factor model of normal personality (McCrae & Costa, 2008). Its items describe a wide variety of negative emotional experiences, such as anxiety, insecurity, and worry. Low scores are interpretable as indicating that the test taker is not prone to such emotions. In addition to heightened negative emotionality, high scorers tend to have a general tendency to catastrophize and to expect the worst to happen. Among the other scales of the MMPI–2–RF, this scale correlates most highly with Dysfunctional Negative Emotions *(RC7)* and is thus included in this strand for interpretation purposes.

Interpretation Guidelines for Negative Emotionality/Neuroticism–Revised *(NEGE-r)* Scores

Content-based interpretation:

$T < 39$	Client reports a below-average level of negative emotional experiences.
$T \geq 65$	Client reports various negative emotional experiences.

Empirically, other individuals with elevations on this scale

- experience various negative emotional experiences, including anxiety, insecurity, and worry
- are inhibited behaviorally because of negative emotions
- are self-critical and guilt prone
- experience intrusive ideation

Additional diagnostic and treatment considerations:

- The presence of personality disorder should be evaluated.
- Emotional distress may motivate the client for treatment.
- Excessive or exclusive focus on negative information is an appropriate treatment target.
- Antianxiety medication could be considered.

Thought Dysfunction Scales

The scales in the Thought Dysfunction domain reflect thinking-related problems that are traditionally associated with psychotic disorders. The key symptom sets in this domain are hallucinations and delusions, and the neo-Kraepelinian category of Schizophrenia certainly comes to mind. It is worth revisiting the paradigm shift described in Chapter 1—that is, the recent movement in the field of psychopathology away from discrete diagnostic categories toward hierarchically organized dimensional constructs. Perhaps more than any other type of psychopathology, psychosis and schizophrenia invoke dichotomous thinking—many people view these as disorders that one either has or does not have. Indeed, it is relatively easy to reconceptualize more common dysfunctions, like anxiety or demoralization, as dimensional constructs; Neuroticism, as represented in the five-factor model of personality, clearly exhibits a normal bell-shaped distribution. However, it is more difficult to see dimensionality in symptoms such as visual or auditory hallucinations or even in delusions of persecution.

The important conceptual work of Harkness and McNulty (1994) in developing the PSY–5 model provided a foundation for rethinking the construct of psychoticism. Briefly, as a broad, overarching construct, *psychoticism* may be thought of dimensionally as reflecting the individual's quality of contact with consensual reality. As an individual difference, this characteristic can certainly be seen as ordinal, and some degree of impairment in connection with consensual reality can be found in many disorders, not just the schizophrenias.

There are just four scales in the Thought Dysfunction domain, including the Higher-Order scale Thought Dysfunction *(THD)*. The two RC Scales, Ideas of Persecution *(RC6)* and Aberrant Experiences *(RC8)*, focus on delusions and hallucinations, respectively. Finally, the PSY–5 scale Psychoticism–Revised *(PSYC-r)* is included.

THOUGHT DYSFUNCTION *(THD)*

THD, with 26 items, is one of the three Higher-Order Scales of the MMPI–2–RF, reflecting the importance and potentially high impact of this type of psychopathology, even though it is less frequent than the other broad types (Internalizing and Externalizing). All of *THD*'s 26 items also appear on either *RC6* or *RC8*. The overall score on *THD* can be seen as an index of the client's level of thought dysfunction. Clinically elevated scores suggest substantial difficulties associated with abnormal thinking processes. More specific interpretive statements are most likely to be derived from *RC6, RC8,* and/or *PSYC-r* (described below). As noted earlier, the Higher-Order Scales were developed primarily through factor analysis of the RC Scales. *THD* was clearly defined by *RC6* and *RC8*.

Interpretation Guidelines for Thought Dysfunction *(THD)* Scores

Content-based interpretation:

T = 65–79	Client's responses indicate significant thought dysfunction.
T ≥ 80	Client's responses indicate serious thought dysfunction.

Empirically, other individuals with elevations on this scale

- experience a broad range of symptoms and difficulties associated with disordered thinking, such as paranoid and nonparanoid delusions, auditory or visual hallucinations, and unrealistic thinking; specific symptom patterns should be reflected in scores on *RC6, RC8,* and *PSYC-r*

Additional diagnostic and treatment considerations:

- The presence of disorders associated with thought dysfunction should be evaluated.
- The client may require inpatient hospitalization.
- The need for antipsychotic medication should be evaluated.

IDEAS OF PERSECUTION *(RC6)*

The original Clinical Scale 6—Paranoia was a broad scale including content reflecting a significant component of demoralization (now measured by *RCd*), an element of cynicism (now measured by *RC3*), and self-referential delusions of persecution by others. It is this last element that was identified as the major distinctive component of *RC6*, which has 17 items reflecting the level of persecutory beliefs held by the test taker. Most of these items are self-referential, rather extreme, and rare in the population (e.g., the belief that one is being followed). Because these items were rarely endorsed in the normative sample, a raw score of only 3 of the 17 items results in a clinical-range *T* score.

RC6 is one of the seven scales routinely identified as having critical content. Thus, all items answered in the scored direction are printed in full in the computer-produced Score Report. In this case, the finding of significant persecutory thinking may require immediate intervention.

Interpretation Guidelines for Ideas of Persecution *(RC6)* Scores

Content-based interpretation:

T = 65–79	Client's responses suggest significant persecutory ideation, such as believing that others are seeking to harm him or her.
T ≥ 80	At this level, the persecutory thinking likely rises to the level of paranoid delusions.

Empirically, other individuals with elevations on this scale

- experience paranoid delusions (if $T \geq 80$)
- are suspicious of and alienated from others
- experience interpersonal difficulties as a result of suspiciousness
- lack insight
- blame others for their own difficulties

Additional diagnostic and treatment considerations:

- The presence of paranoid disorders should be evaluated.
- Persecutory ideas may have a negative impact on the therapeutic relationship and impede treatment.
- The need for inpatient treatment and/or antipsychotic medication should be considered (if $T \geq 80$).

ABERRANT EXPERIENCES *(RC8)*

The 18 items of *RC8* contain content that describes unusual thinking and unusual perceptual experiences. Elevated scores signal the possibility of psychotic disorders, and significant elevations indicate disordered thinking. *RC8* has been designated as one of the seven scales with critical content; thus, when elevated, all items endorsed in the scored direction are printed in full on the computer-produced Score Report. It is important to be mindful of the fact that certain neurological disorders can produce similar symptoms. This is also true for substance use, which at times can produce overtly psychotic symptomatology (and elevations on *RC8*). Thus, the full case history and collateral information should be considered carefully in the interpretation of elevated *RC8* scores.

Interpretation Guidelines for Aberrant Experiences *(RC8)* Scores

Content-based interpretation:

$T = 65–74$	Client reports various unusual thought and perceptual processes.
$T \geq 75$	Client reports a large number of unusual thoughts and perceptions.

Empirically, other individuals with elevations on this scale

- experience thought disorganization
- engage in unrealistic thinking
- believe they have unusual sensory–perceptual abilities
- possibly experience somatic delusions (if Somatic Complaints *[RC1]*, Head Pain Complaints *[HPC]*, or Neurological Complaints *[NUC]* scores are ≥ 65)
- may be experiencing substance-induced psychotic symptoms (if Substance Abuse *[SUB]* score is ≥ 65)
- may experience auditory and/or visual hallucinations and nonpersecutory delusions such as thought broadcasting and mind reading (if $T \geq 80$)
- experience significant impairment in occupational and interpersonal functioning (if $T \geq 80$).

Additional diagnostic and treatment considerations:

- The presence of disorders involving psychotic symptoms should be evaluated.
- Schizophrenia, paranoid type (if $T \geq 75$), should be considered.
- The presence of personality disorders involving unusual thoughts and perceptions should be evaluated.
- Impaired thinking may disrupt treatment.
- Assisting the client in gaining insight about his or her thought dysfunction is an appropriate target for treatment.
- The client may require inpatient treatment (if $T \geq 75$).
- The need for antipsychotic medication should be evaluated (if $T \geq 75$).

PSYCHOTICISM–REVISED *(PSYC-r)*

The 26-item *PSYC-r* is the MMPI–2–RF version of the PSY–5 *PSYC* scale originally developed for the MMPI–2. Its items describe a variety of symptoms associated with thought disturbance. Low scores may be interpreted as indicating orderly, conventional thinking processes without unusual characteristics. Elevated scores suggest, as described earlier, increasing levels of disconnection with consensual reality. More specifically, elevated scores are reflective of unusual thinking, unusual perceptual experiences, and social alienation. In comparing the PSY–5 model to the five-factor model of normal personality, Psychoticism is the only factor with no clear counterpart. Again, the rationale here is that the problems associated with this scale are relatively rare in the population and generally do not emerge in factor analytic studies of nonclinical populations. *PSYC-r* correlates highly (.95) with *THD* in both men and women.

Interpretation Guidelines for Psychoticism–Revised *(PSYC-r)* Scores

Content-based interpretation:

$T < 39$	Client reports no experiences of thought disturbance.
$T \geq 65$	Client reports various experiences associated with thought dysfunction.

Empirically, other individuals with elevations on this scale

- experience unusual thought processes and perceptual phenomena (if $T \geq 65$)
- are alienated from others (if $T \geq 65$)
- engage in unrealistic thinking (if $T \geq 65$)
- present with impaired reality testing (if $T \geq 65$)

Additional diagnostic and treatment considerations:

- The presence of personality disorders characterized by unusual thinking should be evaluated.

Externalizing Scales

The discipline of psychology, broadly, is often defined as the scientific study of thinking, feeling, and behaving, and the three Higher-Order Scales reflect dysfunction in these areas. The Externalizing domain thus addresses maladaptive behaviors, including aggression, acting out, stormy interpersonal relationships, conflicts with society and legal authorities, substance misuse, stealing, lying, and so forth. Traditional diagnostic labels for problems in this domain include *oppositional/defiant disorders, conduct disorders, antisocial personality,* and others. Individuals with elevated scores on the scales in the Externalizing domain are typically described as extroverted, dominant and domineering, aggressive, self-centered, overactive, and impulsive. At times they may exhibit overt aggression or even violent behavior, and a history of legal conflict is characteristic.

One key concept in this domain is *disconstraint,* a deficiency in one's ability to maintain self-control and inhibition of urges and impulses. Disconstraint is one of the most important and predictive factors in human personality. It relates directly to the Conscientiousness factor in the normal five-factor model of personality, and in Tellegen's (1985) theory of personality, disconstraint is one of the three higher-order factors (along with positive emotionality and negative emotionality). Behavior becomes dysfunctional, or maladaptive, in many cases as a result of a failure of normal inhibitory process, such as impulse control, self-control, self-discipline, and so forth.

There are nine scales in the Externalizing domain, including one of the three Higher-Order Scales, Behavioral/Externalizing Dysfunction *(BXD).* As shown in Figure 1.1, under *BXD* are two of the RC Scales (Antisocial Behavior *[RC4]* and Hypomanic Activation *[RC9]*), four Specific Problems Scales (Juvenile Conduct Problems *[JCP],* Substance Abuse *[SUB],* Aggression *[AGG],* and Activation *[ACT]*), and two of the PSY–5 Scales (Aggressiveness–Revised *[AGGR-r]* and Disconstraint—Revised *[DISC-r]*).

BEHAVIORAL/EXTERNALIZING DYSFUNCTION *(BXD)*

As noted, *BXD,* with 23 items, is one of the three Higher-Order Scales of the MMPI–2–RF. Its items include content spanning a range of maladaptive behavioral issues. Core factors within this domain include antisocial personality traits and behaviors, aggressiveness and hyperactivity, and disconstraint or impulse control problems. Taking all of these issues together, *BXD* serves as a broad index of the individual's tendencies toward acting out. Low scores may be interpreted as a higher-than-average level of behavioral constraint, and elevated scores suggest a wide array of externalizing, acting-out behaviors.

Interpretation Guidelines for Behavioral/Externalizing Dysfunction *(BXD)* Scores

Content-based interpretation:

$T < 39$	Client's responses indicate a higher-than-average level of behavioral constraint; he or she is unlikely to engage in externalizing, acting-out behavior.
$T = 65–79$	Client's responses indicate significant externalizing, acting-out behavior, which is likely to have gotten him or her into difficulties.
$T \geq 80$	Client's responses indicate considerable externalizing, acting-out behavior that is very likely to result in marked dysfunction and to have gotten him or her into difficulties.

Empirically, other individuals with elevations on this scale

- exhibit a broad range of behaviors and difficulties associated with undercontrolled behavior (e.g., substance use, criminal history, violent and abusive behavior, poor impulse control); specific patterns are reflected in scores on the Restructured Clinical, Specific Problems, and PSY–5 Scales.

Additional diagnostic and treatment considerations:

- The presence of externalizing disorders should be evaluated.
- Elevations on *BXD* suggest a lack of internal motivation for treatment and high risk for noncompliance.
- Enhancement of self-control is an appropriate target for intervention.

ANTISOCIAL BEHAVIOR *(RC4)*

The 22 items of *RC4* have content focusing on various antisocial behaviors and related family conflict. Low scores are interpretable as indicating a lower-than-average level of antisocial behavior in the past and a lower-than-average risk for the types of problems associated with elevations on this scale. It should be noted that a majority of items on this scale are worded in the past tense, with content related to specific overt antisocial behaviors. Thus, the most accurate interpretation of an elevated score would be that the client reported a history of antisocial behavior. That said, the correlates listed in the second section of the text box below are well established empirically and may be reported with confidence. Two Specific Problems Scales, Juvenile Conduct Problems *(JCP)* and Substance Abuse *(SUB)*, are interpreted as facets of *RC4*.

Interpretation Guidelines for Antisocial Behavior *(RC4)* Scores

Content-based interpretation:

$T < 39$	Client reports a below-average level of past antisocial behavior.
$T \geq 65$	Client reports a significant history of past antisocial behavior.

Empirically, other individuals with elevations on this scale

- have been involved with the criminal justice system
- fail to conform to societal norms and expectations
- have difficulties with individuals in positions of authority
- experience conflictual interpersonal relationships
- are impulsive
- act out when bored
- have antisocial characteristics
- have a history of juvenile delinquency
- engage in substance misuse
- have family problems
- are interpersonally aggressive

Additional diagnostic and treatment considerations:

- The presence of antisocial personality disorder, substance use disorder, and other externalizing disorders should be evaluated.

- Tendencies toward acting out can result in interference with the establishment of a therapeutic relationship, resistance to treatment, and treatment noncompliance.
- Inadequate self-control is an appropriate target for treatment.

JUVENILE CONDUCT PROBLEMS *(JCP)*

The six-item *JCP* scale has content focused on an early history of behavior problems, including stealing, associating with a negative peer group, and exhibiting behavior problems in the school setting. Empirically, elevations on *JCP* are correlated with juvenile delinquency and also with current acting out. If *JCP* is the only elevation among the nine scales in this domain (i.e., if normal-range scores are found on *BXD, RC4, SUB, RC9, AGG, ACT, AGGR-r,* and *DISC-r*), it is likely that the test taker is acknowledging a pattern of behaviors that occurred in childhood or adolescence but no longer occur presently.

Interpretation Guidelines for Juvenile Conduct Problems *(JCP)* Scores

Content-based interpretation:

$T = 65–79$	Client reports a history of problematic behavior at school.
$T \geq 80$	Client reports a history of juvenile conduct problems such as problematic behavior at school, stealing, and being influenced negatively by peers.

Empirically, other individuals with elevations on this scale

- have a history of juvenile delinquency and criminal and antisocial behavior
- experience conflictual interpersonal relationships
- engage in acting-out behavior
- have difficulty with individuals in positions of authority
- have difficulties trusting others

Additional diagnostic and treatment considerations:

- The presence of externalizing disorders, particularly antisocial personality disorder, should be evaluated.

SUBSTANCE ABUSE *(SUB)*

SUB is a seven-item scale with content reflecting past or current substance abuse. Most of the items specifically address alcohol. High scores are correlated with substantially increased risk for substance abuse, including both alcohol and drugs; impaired functioning due to substance use; and a general sensation-seeking trait. The items are face valid and straightforward. Thus, it is possible for an individual who is actively engaged in substance misuse to simply avoid acknowledging this behavior. If the case information includes ongoing substance misuse but the *SUB* score is in the normal range, denial is an appropriate interpretation. Because of the potential imminent risks of substance abuse, the *SUB* scale has been identified as one of the seven scales with critical content; thus, when elevated, all items endorsed in the scored direction are printed in full on the computer-generated Score Report.

Interpretation Guidelines for Substance Abuse *(SUB)* Scores

Content-based interpretation:

T = 65–79	Client reports significant past and current substance abuse.
T ≥ 80	Client reports a significant history of substance abuse, current substance abuse, frequent use of alcohol and drugs, and/or using alcohol to "relax and open up."

Empirically, other individuals with elevations on this scale

- have a history of problematic use of alcohol or drugs
- have had legal problems as a result of substance abuse
- are sensation seeking

Additional diagnostic and treatment considerations:

- The presence of substance use–related disorders should be evaluated.
- Substance abuse should be considered as a focus of treatment.

HYPOMANIC ACTIVATION *(RC9)*

RC9 is a 28-item scale spanning a wide range of emotional characteristics, attitudes, thinking patterns, and behaviors associated with hypomanic activation. Item content reflects heightened energy, racing thoughts, elevated mood, heightened self-regard, excitement seeking, and aggression. Low scores are interpretable as the test taker having reported a below-average level of energy and engagement with the environment. If *RC9* is low and *RC2* is elevated, the combination suggests more pronounced anhedonia and disengagement characteristic of major depression.

Interpretation Guidelines for Hypomanic Activation *(RC9)* Scores

Content-based interpretation:

T < 39	Client reports a below-average level of activation and engagement with his or her environment.
T = 65–74	Client reports an above-average level of activation and engagement with his or her environment.
T ≥ 75	Client reports a considerably above-average level of activation and engagement with his or her environment.

Empirically, other individuals with abnormally high or low scores on this scale (as noted)

- have a very low energy level (if *T* < 35)
- are disengaged from their environment (if *T* < 35)
- are restless and easily bored (if *T* ≥ 65)
- are overactivated, as manifested in poor impulse control, aggression, mood instability, euphoria, excitability, sensation seeking, risk taking, and other forms of undercontrolled behavior (if *T* ≥ 65)
- display narcissistic personality features (if *T* ≥ 65)
- may have a history of symptoms associated with manic or hypomanic episodes (if *T* ≥ 65)

Additional diagnostic and treatment considerations:

- The presence of narcissistic personality disorder should be evaluated.
- The presence of manic or hypomanic episodes, cycling mood, or schizoaffective disorder should be evaluated (if $T \geq 75$ and if Ideas of Persecution *[RC6]* and Aberrant Experiences *[RC8]* scores are ≥ 70).
- Excessive activation may interfere with treatment.
- Mood stabilization, which may warrant consideration of medication and/or hospitalization, is an appropriate focus of treatment.

AGGRESSION *(AGG)*

The nine items on *AGG* have content reflecting physically aggressive behavior. Elevated scores suggest that the individual is likely to have a history of interpersonal abusiveness and violence. Because of the potentially urgent nature of these issues, *AGG* is one of the seven scales designated as having critical content; thus, when elevated, all items endorsed in the scored direction are printed in full in the Score Report to assist in immediate follow-up interviewing. Low scores generally indicate a below-average level of aggressive behavior. It is important to consider scores on the Protocol Validity Scales, particularly indicators of underreporting, before this low-score interpretation can be made with confidence.

Interpretation Guidelines for Aggression *(AGG)* Scores

Content-based interpretation:

$T < 39$	Client reports a below-average level of aggressive behavior.
$T = 65–79$	Client reports engaging in physically aggressive, violent behavior and losing control.
$T \geq 80$	Client reports engaging in physically aggressive, violent behavior, including explosive behavior and physical altercations, and enjoying intimidating others.

Empirically, other individuals with elevations on this scale

- have a history of violent behavior toward others
- are abusive
- experience anger-related problems

Additional diagnostic and treatment considerations:

- The presence of disorders associated with interpersonal aggression should be evaluated.
- Aggression and anger are appropriate targets for intervention.

ACTIVATION *(ACT)*

The eight items on *ACT* describe feelings of heightened excitation and energy level, mood swings, and lack of sleep. Elevated scores are associated with a history of manic or hypomanic episodes and a current high level of activation. Low scores are interpretable as the test taker reporting a lower-than-average level of activation. One should always consider the possibility that the characteristics suggested by high scores are substance induced, which would clearly influence interpretation of data and direction of treatment, so clinicians should look at *ACT* in conjunction with *SUB*.

Interpretation Guidelines for Activation *(ACT)* Scores

Content-based interpretation:

T < 39	Client reports a below-average level of energy and activation.
T = 65–79	Client reports episodes of heightened excitement and energy level.
T ≥ 80	Client reports episodes of heightened excitement and energy level, uncontrollable mood swings, and lack of sleep.

Empirically, other individuals with elevations on this scale

- experience excessive activation
- have a history of manic or hypomanic episodes (if *T* ≥ 80)

Additional diagnostic and treatment considerations:

- The presence of manic or hypomanic episodes or other conditions associated with excessive energy and activation should be evaluated.
- Excessive activation could interfere with treatment.
- The need for mood-stabilizing medication should be considered.

AGGRESSIVENESS–REVISED *(AGGR-r)*

The 18-item *AGGR-r* is a PSY–5 scale that is interpreted within the Externalizing domain of the MMPI–2–RF. The content reflects aggressively assertive behavior. Thus, lower scores suggest the client is passive and submissive, and higher scores are associated with goal-directed, instrumental aggressiveness. *AGG*, described above, suggests physically aggressive and violent behavior, whereas *AGGR-r* is more reflective of social dominance and assertiveness.

Interpretation Guidelines for Aggressiveness–Revised *(AGGR-r)* Scores

Content-based interpretation:

T < 39	Client reports being interpersonally passive and submissive.
T ≥ 65	Client reports being interpersonally aggressive and assertive.

Empirically, other individuals with elevations on this scale

- are overly assertive and socially dominant
- engage in instrumentally aggressive behavior
- believe they have leadership capabilities
- are viewed by others as domineering

Additional diagnostic and treatment considerations:

- The presence of personality disorders should be evaluated.
- Reduction of interpersonally aggressive behavior is an appropriate target for intervention.

DISCONSTRAINT–REVISED *(DISC-r)*

DISC-r, with 20 items, is another of the PSY–5 Scales used interpretively in the Externalizing domain. Its items describe a range of manifestations of undercontrolled, impulsive, disconstrained behavior. High scores are empirically correlated with impulsivity, acting out, and sensation and excitement seeking. Lower scores indicate relatively high levels of behavioral constraint and self-control. As noted earlier, this PSY–5 scale is associated with the Conscientiousness domain of the five-factor model. It is also highly correlated with the *BXD* Higher-Order scale.

Interpretation Guidelines for Disconstraint–Revised *(DISC-r)* Scores

Content-based interpretation:

$T < 39$	Client reports overly constrained behavior.
$T \geq 65$	Client reports various manifestations of disconstrained behavior.

Empirically, other individuals with elevations on this scale

- are behaviorally disconstrained
- engage in acting-out behaviors
- act out impulsively
- are sensation and excitement seeking

Additional diagnostic and treatment considerations:

- Disconstraint suggests lowered motivation for treatment as well as a significant risk for treatment noncompliance.
- Poor impulse control is an appropriate target for treatment.

Interpersonal Functioning Scales

Six of the MMPI–2–RF scales fall into the Interpersonal Functioning domain of the interpretive framework. Clearly, almost all of the Substantive Scales presented thus far have a meaningful impact on the quality of interpersonal relationships, but they have a more compelling association with one of the other major domains (e.g., Internalizing, Externalizing). The six scales in this group share the feature of having primary associations with aspects of interpersonal functioning. A recent article by Franz, Harrop, and McCord (2017) examining these scales may be of particular interest with regard to therapeutic implications.

The first of these scales, Family Problems *(FML)*, addresses conflictual family relationships and alienation from family. Much of this content was originally captured in the original Clinical Scale 4—Psychopathic Deviate in the MMPI–2, and conflictual family relationships are still empirically correlated with Antisocial Behavior *(RC4)* in the MMPI–2–RF. However, dysfunctional family relationships can be conceptualized as causal in a wide range of psychopathologies, such as internalizing and externalizing problems, as well as resultant from a similarly wide range of psychopathologies.

Thus, it is useful to identify the level of family discord as an individual construct, interpreting its meaning in the context of other data.

One of the RC Scales, Cynicism *(RC3)*, has been grouped in this domain interpretively. Cynicism is a key personality trait that has pervasive impact in the life of an individual, with impairment in interpersonal relationships high on the list. Interpersonal Passivity *(IPP)* addresses levels of submissiveness and unassertiveness that are associated with a range of dysfunctions. Finally, the last three scales, Social Avoidance *(SAV)*, Shyness *(SHY)*, and Disaffiliativeness *(DSF)*, provide focused measures supporting the precise assessment of causes and effects of social disengagement.

FAMILY PROBLEMS *(FML)*

The 10 items of *FML* reflect family-related conflict, with regard to both family of origin and current family constellation; more specifically, most of the items can refer to either, and a small number specify family of origin. The scale assesses a range of negative family experiences, including excessive quarreling, dislike of family members, feelings of being unappreciated, and feelings of being unsupported in times of need. High scores indicate poor family relationships, conflicts with family members, negative feelings toward family, and blame of family members for one's own difficulties. Low scores indicate that the client reported a home environment that was relatively nonconflictual. As noted earlier, family problems can be causal contributors to a range of both internalizing and externalizing psychopathologies, and many psychopathological conditions contribute causally to family conflict.

Interpretation Guidelines for Family Problems *(FML)* Scores

Content-based interpretation:

$T < 39$	Client reports a relatively conflict-free past and current family environment.
$T = 65–79$	Client reports conflictual family relationships and lack of support from family members.
$T \geq 80$	Client reports conflictual family relationships and lack of support from family members. Negative family attitudes and experiences include having frequent quarrels, disliking family members, feeling unappreciated by family members, and feeling that family members cannot be counted on in times of need.

Empirically, other individuals with elevations on this scale

- have family conflicts
- experience poor family functioning
- have strong negative feelings about family members
- blame family members for their own difficulties

Additional diagnostic and treatment considerations:

- Family problems are an appropriate target for intervention.

CYNICISM *(RC3)*

The 15-item *RC3* has content reflecting a negative view of human nature. High scores suggest that the test taker has negative views about the motives and intentions of other people in general, believing that others cannot be trusted and are looking out for their own interests. Low scores reflect the basic belief that other people are mainly well intentioned and trustworthy. The misanthropic attitudes included here are non-self-referential in that they refer to people in general, in comparison with Ideas of Persecution *(RC6)*, which contains self-referential items suggesting that the test taker is specifically being singled out for mistreatment.

Cynicism is a high-impact personality trait in many ways. From a behavioral health perspective, it correlates with coronary heart disease and other physical problems. In a variety of stressful occupations, including both public safety personnel and health care professionals, cynicism is associated with proneness to occupational burnout and attrition.

Interpretation Guidelines for Cynicism *(RC3)* Scores

Content-based interpretation:

$T < 39$	Client describes others as well intentioned and trustworthy and disavows cynical beliefs about them.
$T \geq 65$	Client reports having cynical beliefs about others, being distrustful of others, and believing others look out only for their own interests.

Empirically, other individuals with elevations on this scale

- are hostile toward and feel alienated from others
- are distrustful of others
- have negative interpersonal experiences

Additional diagnostic and treatment considerations:

- The presence of personality disorders characterized by feelings of mistrust and hostility toward others should be evaluated.
- Cynicism is likely to impede the development of a therapeutic relationship.
- Lack of trust in others may be an appropriate target for treatment.

INTERPERSONAL PASSIVITY *(IPP)*

IPP, with 10 items, has content describing submissive and unassertive behavior, failure to stand up for oneself, lack of strong opinions, and lack of desire to be in charge. Thus, people with high scores are described as passive, submissive, and behaviorally overcontrolled. Low *IPP* scores suggest that the test-taker sees himself or herself as having leadership abilities but is likely to be perceived by others as domineering. In a recent study comparing the Interpersonal Functioning Scales with the Computerized Adaptive Test of Personality Disorder (CAT–PD; Simms et al., 2011), *IPP* had strong negative correlations with Exhibitionism, Hostile Aggression, Rudeness, and Domineering (Franz et al., 2017).

Interpretation Guidelines for Interpersonal Passivity *(IPP)* Scores

Content-based interpretation:

$T < 39$	Client describes himself or herself as having strong opinions, standing up for himself or herself, being assertive and direct, and/or being able to lead others.
$T = 65$–69	Client reports being unassertive.
$T \geq 80$	Client reports being unassertive and submissive, not liking to be in charge, failing to stand up for himself or herself, and being ready to give in to others.

Empirically, other individuals with abnormally high or low scores on this scale (as noted)

- believe themselves to have leadership capabilities but are likely to be viewed by others as domineering, self-centered, and possibly grandiose (if $T < 39$)
- are passive and submissive in interpersonal relationships (if $T \geq 65$)
- are overcontrolled (if $T \geq 65$)

Additional diagnostic and treatment considerations:

- The presence of disorders characterized by passive–submissive behavior such as dependent personality disorder should be evaluated.
- The presence of features associated with narcissistic personality disorder should be evaluated (if $T \leq 38$).

SOCIAL AVOIDANCE *(SAV)*

The content of the 10-item *SAV*, as its name indicates, focuses on a preference to avoid social situations and on lack of enjoyment of social events. High scores suggest social introversion, difficulties in forming and maintaining close relationships, and emotional constriction. Low scores suggest the opposite interpretation, including gregariousness and enjoyment of social situations. When *SAV* is elevated and *SHY* is not, social avoidance as a personality disposition is more likely than social anxiety. The highest CAT–PD correlations with *SAV* in the Franz et al. (2017) study were Social Withdrawal, Exhibitionism (negative), and Anhedonia.

Interpretation Guidelines for Social Avoidance *(SAV)* Scores

Content-based interpretation:

$T < 39$	Client reports enjoying social situations and events.
$T = 65$–79	Client reports not enjoying social events and avoiding social situations.
$T \geq 80$	Client reports not enjoying social events and avoiding social situations, including parties and other events where crowds are likely to gather.

Empirically, other individuals with abnormally high or low scores on this scale (as noted)

- are likely to be perceived as outgoing and gregarious (if $T < 39$)
- are introverted (if $T \geq 65$)
- have difficulty forming close relationships (if $T \geq 65$)
- are emotionally restricted (if $T \geq 65$)

Additional diagnostic and treatment considerations:

- The presence of disorders associated with social avoidance, including avoidant personality disorder, should be evaluated.
- Intervention should target difficulties associated with social avoidance.

SHYNESS *(SHY)*

The content of the seven-item *SHY* scale focuses on experiencing social anxiety, being easily embarrassed, and feeling uncomfortable around other people. High scores suggest social introversion, inhibition, and anxiety, particularly in social situations. Low scores are interpreted as reflecting the absence of social anxiety, which is a normal-range personality characteristic. The highest CAT–PD correlates (Franz et al., 2017) were Social Withdrawal and Anxiousness. The test authors suggest that low *SHY* scores may be consistent with conversion disorder or psychopathy, depending on other characteristics also present.

Interpretation Guidelines for Shyness *(SHY)* Scores

Content-based interpretation:

$T < 39$	Client reports little or no social anxiety.
$T \geq 65$	Client reports being shy, easily embarrassed, and uncomfortable around others.

Empirically, other individuals with elevations on this scale

- are socially introverted and inhibited
- are anxious and nervous in social situations
- are generally anxious

Additional diagnostic and treatment considerations:

- The presence of social phobia should be evaluated.
- Intervention should target anxiety in social situations.

DISAFFILIATIVENESS *(DSF)*

DSF has six items with content describing an individual who dislikes people, dislikes being around others, has never had a close friend, and prefers being alone. High scores are associated with being asocial, and extremely high scores ($T = 100$) may indicate a schizoid personality disorder. The highest CAT–PD correlates were Emotional Detachment, Mistrust, Anhedonia, Social Withdrawal, and Callousness. Thus, a commonality across *SAV, SHY*, and *DSF* is a high correlation with Social Withdrawal, which is essentially overt behavior. The differences in underlying dispositional factors that may motivate social withdrawal are that *SAV* reflects introversion and emotional constriction, *SHY* reflects social anxiety, and *DSF* reflects detachment and dislike of people.

Interpretation Guidelines for Disaffiliativeness *(DSF)* Scores

Content-based interpretation:

T = 65–79	Client reports disliking people and being around them.
T = 80–99	Client reports disliking people and being around them, preferring to be alone.
T = 100	Client reports disliking people and being around them, preferring to be alone and never having had a close relationship.

Empirically, other individuals with elevations on this scale

- are seen as asocial

Additional diagnostic and treatment considerations:

- The presence of schizoid personality disorder should be evaluated (if *T* = 100).
- Extreme difficulties with close relationships may impede the process of forming a therapeutic alliance.

Interest Scales

The MMPI and MMPI–2 included Basic Scale 5—Masculinity/Femininity. Scale 5 was originally developed for the purpose of assessing sexual orientation during a time in history when homosexuality was grouped with psychopathology syndromes. The scale failed in this goal and almost immediately became interpreted instead as a measure of vocational, avocational, and general interest patterns stereotypically associated with each gender (Graham, 2011). In the restructuring of the Clinical Scales (Tellegen et al., 2003), Scale 5 was decomposed and reconstructed as two different scales free of gender connotations: Aesthetic–Literary Interests *(AES)* and Mechanical–Physical Interests *(MEC)*. As these are not measures of psychopathology, they are briefly described here without interpretation text boxes. If scores on both scales are notably low, the pervasive lack of general interests suggested may be consistent with anhedonia and may contribute to the characterization of a major depressive disorder.

AESTHETIC–LITERARY INTERESTS *(AES)*

The seven items of *AES* describe interests of an artistic nature as reflected in activities or occupations related to writing, music, or theater. In addition to directly indicating these interest patterns by item content, high scores are associated with empathy and with being sensitive and responsive to sensory experiences. Low scores (< 39) suggest no interest in aesthetic–literary activities.

MECHANICAL–PHYSICAL INTERESTS *(MEC)*

MEC, with nine items, describes interests in activities or occupations of a mechanical or physical nature such as building or fixing things; outdoor activities such as farming, hunting, or fishing; and sports activities. In addition to directly indicating these interest patterns by item content, high scores are associated with adventurousness and sensation seeking. Low scores (< 39) indicate no interest in mechanical–physical activities.

Interpretive Framework 5

This chapter outlines explicitly a step-by-step approach to interpretation that should facilitate the development of mastery very quickly in emerging clinicians and promote consistency of Minnesota Multiphasic Personality Inventory—2—Restructured Form (MMPI–2–RF) test interpretation within the field. With regard to enhancing consistency across examiners and MMPI–2–RF interpretations, the test authors recommend a specific framework for approaching the test data. This framework is depicted graphically in Figure 1.1, and it is also reflected clearly in the scores-by-domain presentation of the Score Report and in the MMPI–2–RF Interpretation Worksheet (described below). Table 5.1 reproduces the overall framework in brief tabular form.

As noted earlier, the overall method is a two-pass approach; in the first pass, you scan relatively rapidly through all of the scales by hierarchical scale sets, and in the slower, more methodical second pass, you go back through all of the scales by domain. Referring again to Figure 1.1, in the first pass you basically go from top to bottom, and in the second pass you go from left to right, one domain at a time, making notes on all elevated (and some low) scale scores. During the second pass, as you develop interpretive statements that apply to the case, you also make notes as you go regarding diagnostic implications and treatment recommendations.

In Chapter 6, I use this interpretive strategy to go through an actual case. In that context, I reproduce a full Score Report, and it will be useful at points

http://dx.doi.org/10.1037/0000074-006
Assessment Using the MMPI–2–RF, by D. M. McCord

TABLE 5.1

Interpretive Framework for Approaching the Test Data

Scale	Sources of Information
I. Protocol Validity Scales	
a. Content nonresponsiveness	Cannot Say *(CNS)*, Variable Response Inconsistency *(VRIN-r)*, True Response Inconsistency *(TRIN-r)*
b. Overreporting	Infrequent Responses *(F-r)*, Infrequent Psychopathology Responses *(Fp-r)*, Infrequent Somatic Responses *(Fs)*, Symptom Validity *(FBS-r)*, Response Bias *(RBS)*
c. Underreporting	Uncommon Virtues *(L-r)*, Adjustment Validity *(K-r)*
II. Substantive Scales	
a. Somatic/Cognitive	Somatic Complaints *(RC1)*, Malaise *(MLS)*, Gastrointestinal Complaints *(GIC)*, Head Pain Complaints *(HPC)*, Neurological Complaints *(NUC)*, Cognitive Complaints *(COG)*
b. Internalizing	Emotional/Internalizing Dysfunction *(EID)*, Demoralization *(RCd)*, Low Positive Emotions *(RC2)*, Dysfunctional Negative Emotions *(RC7)*, Suicidal/Death Ideation *(SUI)*, Helplessness/Hopelessness *(HLP)*, Self-Doubt *(SFD)*, Inefficacy *(NFC)*, Stress/Worry *(STW)*, Anxiety *(AXY)*, Anger Proneness *(ANP)*, Behavior-Restricting Fears *(BRF)*, Multiple Specific Fears *(MSF)*, Negative Emotionality/Neuroticism–Revised *(NEGE-r)*, Introversion/Low Positive Emotionality–Revised *(INTR-r)*
c. Thought Dysfunction	Thought Dysfunction *(THD)*, Ideas of Persecution *(RC6)*, Aberrant Experiences *(RC8)*, Psychoticism–Revised *(PSYC-r)*
d. Externalizing	Behavioral/Externalizing Dysfunction *(BXD)*, Antisocial Behavior *(RC4)*, Hypomanic Activation *(RC9)*, Juvenile Conduct Problems *(JCP)*, Substance Abuse *(SUB)*, Activation *(ACT)*, Aggression *(AGG)*, Aggressiveness–Revised *(AGG-r)*, Disconstraint–Revised *(DISC-r)*
e. Interpersonal Functioning	Family Problems *(FML)*, Cynicism *(RC3)*, Interpersonal Passivity *(IPP)*, Shyness *(SHY)*, Social Avoidance *(SAV)*, Disaffiliativeness *(DSF)* (Introversion/Low Positive Emotionality–Revised *[INTR-r]*)

Note. Adapted from *Interpreting the MMPI–2–RF* by Yossef S. Ben-Porath.

to refer to this report as I develop the interpretive process (see Figure 6.1). You may also want to download one of the sample MMPI–2–RF score reports from the Pearson website so you can have it handy as you go through Chapter 5 without having to go back and forth with the Chapter 6 example.

Similarly, a key tool I will use in interpretation is the MMPI–2–RF Interpretation Worksheet, a four-page interactive PDF document. Although this worksheet was developed by the test authors and is copyrighted, it is free for use, downloadable from the University of Minnesota Press Test Division website as well as the Pearson website, and its use is strongly encouraged. The Interpretation Worksheet is also reproduced in Chapter 6 as part of the case example (Figure 6.2), and I refer to it as appropriate in the current chapter. If you have not yet downloaded a copy of the Interpretation Worksheet, this would be a good time to do it.

First Pass

Almost all experienced MMPI users follow the basic approach of scanning through the graphic presentation of test results to get an overview of the case and then cycling back through the data in a more systematic, targeted second pass, guided in part by the initial orientation. Whether the test has been computer scored or hand scored, the key data are presented in graphic form on five profile sheets (see pages 2–6 of the sample Score Report presented in Figure 6.1). In the first pass, you spend a minute or so with each of these profile sheets, looking for key markers and highlights and mentally prioritizing and organizing your findings. It is good practice to first be mindful of the most salient framing characteristics of the case, including age, gender, key demographic data, current life circumstances, and reason for referral. Then go through the five profile sheets in the standard order.

PROTOCOL VALIDITY SCALES

When checking the Protocol Validity Scale results (page 2 of the Score Report), you should quickly consider four basic questions. First, was the client responsive? Check the Cannot Say *(CNS)* count. If it is ≥ 15, then it is likely that some of the scales are not valid, and this becomes an important consideration; the focus should be on the Response % under each scale, even in the first pass, to avoid misinterpretations. *CNS* scores from 1 to 14 also require attentiveness to the scale-level Response %, but most scales should be interpretable.

Second, did the client respond in a consistent manner? Check Variable Response Inconsistency *(VRIN-r)* and True Response Inconsistency *(TRIN-r)*. If either *T* score is ≥ 80, the protocol is invalid due to inconsistency.

Third, are there indications of overreporting psychopathology? Check Infrequent Responses *(F-r)*, Infrequent Psychopathology Responses *(Fp-r)*, Infrequent Somatic Responses *(Fs)*, Symptom Validity *(FBS)*, and Response Bias *(RBS)*. If *F-r* = 120 or *Fp-r* ≥ 100, the protocol is invalid due to overreporting. If *T* scores on any of the other three scales are ≥ 100, there are indications of specific forms of overreporting.

Fourth, are there indications of underreporting psychopathology? Check Uncommon Virtues *(L-r)* and Adjustment Validity *(K-r)*. If $L\text{-}r \geq 80$ or $K\text{-}r \geq 70$, then there are tendencies toward underreporting that need to be considered in understanding the Substantive Scales.

HIGHER-ORDER AND RESTRUCTURED CLINICAL SCALES

The broadest level Higher-Order (H-O) and the midlevel Restructured Clinical (RC) Scales are presented in this profile sheet (page 3 of the Score Report). The left-most three scales are the H-O Scales and are very important overall indicators of psychopathology. In the first pass, see first whether any of these are elevated ($T \geq 65$) and then check the relative order of elevation. This information gives you an important general overview of the types of issues the case presents. As you think about the ultimate narrative in your formal psychological report, you will most likely begin with a discussion of issues reflected by the highest of these three H-O Scales (if clinically elevated).

The nine RC Scales are presented next. Again, look for elevations ($T \geq 65$) and for notably low scores. Consider whether the pattern of elevations on the RC Scales is consistent with what you saw in the H-O Scales or adds new information. Also note that Ideas of Persecution *(RC6)* and Aberrant Experiences *(RC8)* are two of the seven scales designated by the test authors as having critical content. If elevated, items endorsed in the scored direction are printed in full; even in this first pass, you would most likely want to view the item-level information (page 8 of the Score Report) to see the actual content of the items that produced these elevations, as this might well influence your overall organization of the data in your report.

SOMATIC/COGNITIVE AND INTERNALIZING SCALES

The Somatic/Cognitive and Internalizing Scales are reported in the first of the two profile sheets that present Specific Problems (SP) Scales, the narrowest in focus of the MMPI–2–RF scales (page 4 of the Score Report). This profile sheet includes five Somatic/Cognitive SP Scales and nine Internalizing SP Scales. Again, note elevations (≥ 65) and low scores, paying special attention to any of the scales designated by test authors as having critical content. On this profile sheet three of the seven Critical Scales appear: Suicidal/Death Ideation (*SUI*; bolded), Helplessness/Hopelessness *(HLP)*, and Anxiety *(AXY)*. Quickly check item-level information on Score Report page 8 to see the content of items endorsed on these scales.

EXTERNALIZING, INTERPERSONAL FUNCTIONING, AND INTEREST SCALES

The four Externalizing SP Scales and the five Interpersonal Functioning SP Scales, as well as the two Interest Scales, are included in a single profile sheet (page 5 of the Score Report). Two of the seven scales with critical content are on this profile sheet,

Substance Abuse *(SUB)* and Aggression *(AGG)*; if elevated, review item content on Score Report page 8.

PERSONALITY PSYCHOPATHOLOGY FIVE SCALES

The Personality Psychopathology Five (PSY–5) Scales, developed originally by Harkness, McNulty, and Ben-Porath (1995) and revised for the MMPI–2–RF (Harkness, Finn, McNulty, & Shields, 2012; Harkness et al., 2014), are included in a single profile sheet (page 6 of the Score Report). A full discussion of the theoretical importance of the PSY–5 Scales is beyond the scope of this practical book, but I strongly encourage you to read one or more of the source citations listed above. Essentially, these constructs are the five primary dimensions of personality and psychopathology, providing a linkage between the MMPI–2–RF and other current models of psychopathology.

In your first pass, you should consider the PSY–5 Scales as broad dimensions, and they will provide you with a second opinion, so to speak, with regard to your other data. For example, if Emotional/Internalizing Dysfunction *(EID)* was elevated and clearly higher than Thought Dysfunction *(THD)* and Behavioral/Externalizing Dysfunction *(BXD)*, you would expect to see similar elevations on Negative Emotionality/Neuroticism–Revised *(NEGE-r)* and/or Introversion/Low Positive Emotionality–Revised *(INTR-r)*, with lower scores on Aggressiveness–Revised *(AGGR-r)* and Disconstraint–Revised *(DISC-r)*. If *THD* is elevated, then Psychoticism–Revised *(PSYC-r)* should also be elevated. Any discrepancies between the PSY–5 scores and your broad and midlevel MMPI–2–RF scales could be explored by means of narrower facets assessed by the SP Scales. In your second pass, you embed the PSY–5 Scales within the appropriate domains, where they provide additional information at the level of the SP Scales.

As noted above, it is important even in your brief first pass to examine the item-level information presented on page 8 of the Score Report. This page provides the full text of any items that were omitted, including a listing of the scales on which these items would have been scored. This detailed information can be very important in understanding the impact of *CNS* scores > 0. The next section addresses the seven scales designated by the test authors has having critical content. If any of these scales is elevated, the full text of all items endorsed in the scored direction is presented, along with the direction of the scored response, the percentage of the normative sample endorsing this item, and if a comparison group has been designated, the percentage of that group endorsing the item. The final section provides the same data for any scales that were designated by the user as warranting item-level information.

At the end of the first pass, you should have a clear sense of the context of the case and of the broad pattern of test data. You then approach the second pass with a clear sense of direction, well oriented to the pattern of scores. This overall orientation ultimately facilitates the production of a coherent, clear narrative. At the same time, it is important to avoid premature closure and to remain open-minded as you go through the second pass, which provides a more thorough, careful, and systematic approach to the data.

Second Pass

In the second pass, your goal is to prepare an Interpretation Worksheet that contains all of the relevant MMPI–2–RF information, including your scale-based interpretations, hypotheses, diagnostic speculations, and treatment ideas. The Interpretation Worksheet is an intermediate product between the Score Report and your own narrative psychological report that you prepare for the end user. Although you used the graphic profile sheets as your primary input data in the first pass, in the second pass your primary input data are assembled for you in the scores-by-domain format, which appears on page 7 of the Score Report. The *CNS* raw count plus all 51 scale scores are reported on this single page in the domain order that you will use in completing the Interpretation Worksheet (which is the same order in which scales are presented in Chapters 3 and 4).

Because the Interpretation Worksheet is an interactive PDF, I suggest that you print a hard copy of page 7, the scores-by-domain report, and then have the Interpretation Worksheet active on your computer. Note that if you have used a comparison group, which is strongly recommended, you will need to have the profile sheets handy as well because comparison group data are not included on Score Report page 7. The first step, then, is to transfer the scores from the printout to the appropriate blanks on the Interpretation Worksheet; some clinicians prefer to do this all at once, whereas others transfer scores a section at a time.

PROTOCOL VALIDITY SCALES

The first page of the Interpretation Worksheet contains the Protocol Validity indicators. Fill in the blanks for the three content nonresponsiveness scores, the five overreporting scores, and the two underreporting scores. Then turn to Chapter 3 and go through all 10 of the tables in that chapter, which are in the same order as the Interpretation Worksheet. Consider the score for each indicator, and derive from the table the appropriate interpretive language. In many cases, this could be a single, simple sentence for the entire section. For example, if *CNS* = 0 and neither *VRIN-r* nor *TRIN-r* is elevated, you could type, "There are no indications of nonresponsiveness." This is not exactly the way you will express this in your final report for the end user, but in this intermediate step it serves the purpose.

Then consider the overreporting and underreporting indicators. Again, in many cases in typical clinical settings, cooperative clients are striving to provide an accurate self-report, and your sentence may very well be, "There is no evidence of overreporting (or underreporting)." Generally, the narrative you take from Chapter 3 to include in your worksheet most often comes from the second column (Validity Issue), but you may find it useful to include some of the reasons and implications from Column 3 (Possible Reasons) or 4 (Interpretive Issues), depending on the context of the case. Remember, this is your worksheet, really just for your own use, so your wording does not have to be in final form.

SUBSTANTIVE SCALES

The next two pages (pages 2 and 3) of the Interpretation Worksheet focus on the Substantive Scales of the MMPI–2–RF, going through the five domains. Again, in this step you are primarily moving numerical scores from Score Report page 7 to the worksheet, and then using Chapter 4 to provide narrative interpretation of those scores. It is most effective to complete the worksheet in order (i.e., Somatic/Cognitive first, then Internalizing, and so forth), even though your ordering of information is likely to change as you move narrative from the worksheet into your final report. In your psychological report, it is almost always best to begin your narrative with the most important issues so that they get the most emphasis. Also, as you extract interpretive statements from the text boxes in Chapter 4, consider any diagnostic implications and treatment considerations that are suggested for the scale in focus. The last two sections of the Interpretation Worksheet (page 4) are included to allow accumulation of such comments as you go through the data.

You will find in following this standard procedure that your paragraphs for each of the five major substantive domains are often logical, coherent, and appropriate for cut-and-paste transfer to your final psychological report. In contrast, the Diagnostic Considerations and Treatment Considerations sections of the Interpretation Worksheet (page 4) are best seen as working notes or bullet lists to be integrated later into the final section of your full psychological report.

Somatic/Cognitive Domain

The first substantive area of the Interpretation Worksheet addresses the Somatic/Cognitive domain. Transfer the scores, and then begin with the text boxes in Chapter 4 to construct narrative for the Somatic/Cognitive Dysfunction section of the worksheet. In this domain, Somatic Complaints *(RC1)* is the broadest; thus, if it is elevated, always start with the more general interpretive comments associated with *RC1*. If *RC1* is not elevated, then start with the highest elevation among the other five scales. Go in order of descending elevation for all scores ≥ 65.

Note that Cognitive Complaints *(COG)* is a relatively independent, transdomain construct. The conceptual focus of this domain is somatization, and cognitive problems can certainly occur in this context. However, they can also occur as manifestations of anxiety, depressivity, and other internalizing processes, or as aspects of psychotic disorders, or in the context of externalizing dysfunction such as attention deficits and hyperactivity. Thus, although this section of the worksheet is a perfectly good place to record the appropriate narrative interpretation for a given elevation on *COG*, it may be most appropriate to integrate this narrative into sections of your final report that focus on primary psychopathology patterns, other than somatization, with which *COG* may be most closely associated in the specific case.

Internalizing Domain

The second substantive area of the Interpretation Worksheet addresses the Internalizing domain. This is the domain that is most elaborated in the MMPI–2–RF assessment model, and it includes the forms of dysfunction experienced by a majority of clients in most outpatient settings. As a reminder, of the 40 scales on the MMPI–2–RF that measure psychopathology constructs, 15 fall within the Internalizing domain. After transferring all 15 scale scores to the Emotional Dysfunction section of the worksheet, approach this domain hierarchically. If the Higher-Order scale Emotional/Internalizing Dysfunction *(EID)* is elevated, draw appropriate interpretive statements from the text box and type them on the Interpretation Worksheet. More specifically, in this text box there are three elevation-based content statements; if one of these fits the score, use that sentence (almost exactly) as the opening sentence of this section. Although there are numerous empirical correlates also provided, it is usually best to use the midlevel and specific scales in this hierarchy for detailed interpretation.

Moving next to the midlevel scales, remember that in this domain there is a body of current research that describes a three-factor model of internalizing dysfunction (Demoralization/Distress, Depressivity/Anhedonia, Anxiety/Fear), with midlevel scales Demoralization *(RCd)*, Low Positive Emotions *(RC2)*, and Dysfunctional Negative Emotions *(RC7)* reflecting those three factors. Thus, following the opening sentence drawn from *EID*, the recommended approach is to consider elevations ≥ 65 among these three scales and begin the interpretation with the one that is most highly elevated. Once the starting point is identified, use the appropriate elevation-based content statement from the text box, and then consider elaborating with the empirical correlates listed in the text box.

Next, go through the narrow facets associated with that RC Scale, following the order on the Interpretation Worksheet. Again, start with the appropriate elevation-based content statement, and then add empirical correlates as appropriate. If either of the other two RC Scales is elevated, treat it similarly, in descending order. You will find that the elevation-based content statement is most often unique to that scale and will add new information to your report. However, the empirical correlates overlap considerably, and once included there is no need for redundancy. Note that this standard procedure will capture all elevated SP (and PSY–5) Scales as long as the parent RC Scale is clinically elevated.

Once you go through this process, there may be some elevated SP or PSY–5 Scales under a parent RC Scale that was not elevated. For example, you may have started with *RCd* and its facets, then *RC2* and its single facet, but *RC7* was not elevated. Thus, you would not yet have considered the six facets under *RC7*. Recall that each of these Substantive Scales has independent validity and may be interpreted even if its hierarchical parent scale is not elevated. Thus, at this point the procedure is to check for any elevated facet scales you have not yet included in the interpretation. Perhaps, for example, Stress/Worry *(STW)* is elevated, even though *RC7* is not. You should review the text box for *STW* and consider including its elevation-determined content statement and possibly some correlates. This information may fit your report best in the context of other narrative text in this paragraph. Alternatively, you may want to conclude this internalizing paragraph with an "In addition . . ." statement that allows the inclusion of all facets not yet addressed. As a reminder, diagnostic and treatment considerations drawn from the text boxes can be accumulated in the last two sections of the Interpretation Worksheet as you go through the five domains.

Thought Dysfunction Domain

The third domain is Thought Dysfunction, with just four scales. First, interpret the Higher-Order scale Thought Dysfunction *(THD)* in the Thought Dysfunction section of the Interpretation Worksheet, beginning with the appropriate elevation-based content statement from the text box. Although empirical correlates are presented, it is most often best to include those under the remaining scales in this domain. Then consider Ideas of Persecution *(RC6)*, Aberrant Experiences *(RC8)*, and Psychoticism–Revised *(PSYC-r)* according to their relative elevations. For each clinically elevated scale, include its content-based statement and then add empirical correlates. As noted previously, it is useful to make notes in the final two sections of the worksheet of any diagnostic and treatment considerations that are included in the text boxes for elevated scales (or that come to mind as you consider the scale data in the broader context of the case).

Externalizing Domain

The fourth domain is Externalizing, with nine scales. This domain, like the Internalizing domain, is fully elaborated with a three-level hierarchy. First listed in the Behavioral Dysfunction section of the Interpretation Worksheet is Behavioral/Externalizing Dysfunction *(BXD)*, one of the three Higher-Order Scales of the MMPI–2–RF. At the next lower level are two scales, Antisocial Behavior *(RC4)* and Hypomanic Activation *(RC9)*. *RC4* has two underlying SP Scales, and *RC9* has two SP Scales and two PSY–5 Scales at the facet level. Following standard procedure, if *BXD* is elevated, add the appropriate elevation-determined content statement to the Behavioral Dysfunction section of the worksheet. Then consider *RC4* and *RC9* in terms of clinical elevation and relative order. Address the RC Scale itself, with the content statement and correlates, and then all elevated underlying facets. Then address the second RC scale, if elevated, and any elevated facets. Finally, be sure that all elevated facet scales have been addressed, even if parent scales are not elevated. Note diagnostic and treatment considerations as appropriate.

Interpersonal Functioning Domain

The fifth major domain is Interpersonal Functioning. This domain is organized somewhat differently in that there is no formal internal hierarchical organization. The scales are ordered generally in terms of breadth of scope. The first scale, Family Problems *(FML)*, is the broadest in scope, and it correlates with more psychopathology constructs from all other domains than do any of the other Interpersonal Functioning Scales, and causality can be in either direction or both. However, these six scales should be interpreted on the basis of relative elevation. For each elevated scale, type the content-based scale and then a sentence noting key empirical correlates in the Interpersonal Functioning section of the worksheet. The narrative paragraph constructed in this manner is often coherent and relevant as an additional perspective on the client. These interpersonal characteristics may directly reflect issues noted in the other domains, and the connection may be mentioned here. This paragraph is often an appropriate ending to the MMPI–2–RF section of the full psychological report.

INTEREST SCALES

As noted at the end of Chapter 4, the two Interest Scales are rarely key aspects of the case and are not relevant in most clinical assessments. One exception that occurs with some frequency is for individuals experiencing significant anhedonia, with elevations on Low Positive Emotions *(RC2)* or Introversion/Low Positive Emotions–Revised *(INTR-r)* and scores on both Interest Scales notably low (< 40). A pervasive lack of interest in vocational and avocational activities reflected by the Interest Scales can be interpreted as further evidence of, or effects of, anhedonia.

Integration Into the Narrative Report

The final completed Interpretation Worksheet can now provide narrative information to be transferred into your full psychological report. The first paragraph should address the Protocol Validity issues. Although your internal process involves 10 distinct questions and takes the full first page of the Interpretation Worksheet, the final narrative is usually a short, succinct, two- or three-sentence paragraph that summarizes for the end user your overall validity conclusions. When all validity indicators are in the valid range, a typical opening paragraph for your interpretation would be something like the following:

> This client has produced a valid and interpretable MMPI–2–RF protocol, reflecting a thoughtful and cooperative approach to the assessment. Thus, her scores on the various clinical and personality scales are likely to provide an accurate description of her overall psychological functioning.

Variations on this text would deal with tendencies to be inconsistent or to overreport or underreport psychopathology, with appropriate caveats.

The next paragraph of the narrative report is dependent on the broad pattern of data. Specifically, the formal recommendation of the test authors is that the first four domains should be considered as candidates for initial focus, with the decision based on relative elevation. As you prepared the Interpretation Worksheet, you wrote a primary narrative paragraph under each of the domains that is most likely a coherent, orderly, well-constructed segment of writing that can be transferred intact to the narrative report. For example, if *EID* was elevated and was the highest of the three Higher-Order Scales and higher than Somatic Complaints *(RC1)*, then your full narrative Emotional Dysfunction paragraph can be cut and pasted. The other three sections (Somatic/Cognitive Dysfunction, Thought Dysfunction, and Behavioral Dysfunction) can then be pasted in order of relative elevation, followed by the Interpersonal Functioning paragraph. You can then quickly and easily edit this full narrative and add transition sentences (e.g., "A third major area of concern is . . .").

The use of the accumulated diagnostic considerations from the next-to-last section of the Interpretation Worksheet is largely dependent on context. You would be mixing paradigms here, of course. As was described in Chapter 1, the MMPI–2–RF reflects a paradigm change in theoretical psychopathology, essentially an abandonment of the traditional neo-Kraepelinian categorical model in favor of current models based on hierarchical structures of dimensional constructs ranging from relatively broad to relatively narrow in scope. Your goal is not to place the individual into a category but rather to describe him or her as accurately as possible, considering the full array of constructs. So, at the end, why would you now want to use that rich descriptive information to simply place the person in a predefined category, a process that inevitably involves ignoring some of his or her actual characteristics while simultaneously suggesting the existence of other characteristics that actually are not present? You may not actually have to do this, and certainly you should consider the wisdom, and any potential benefit to the client, of assigning a *Diagnostic and Statistical Manual of Mental Disorders (DSM)* or *International Classification of Diseases* (ICD) diagnostic label if it is not necessary.

However, these are the two prevailing systems of diagnosis in our field, and in many settings it is important to comply, perhaps for reimbursement or other bureaucratic processes. So the inclusion of the diagnostically relevant data in this section of the Interpretation Worksheet can facilitate the process of formal *DSM* or ICD diagnosis if necessary. Your working notes can include specific diagnostic labels that might fit the case, as well as specific symptoms that meet formal criteria. As you record the diagnosis in your report, justifying it with specific data, I encourage you to consider for a moment the basic artificiality of the diagnostic category, one that was human-made and included in the manual by majority vote of a committee, ultimately for (possibly very legitimate) bureaucratic purposes. Nature is more accurately reflected as hierarchically organized dimensional constructs. Make every effort to avoid thinking that the result of your assessment work is to "discover" the underlying "disorder" that the person "has"; that was the old paradigm. Your empirically driven descriptions of the individual across the five primary domains are the essential result of the assessment.

The final section of the Interpretation Worksheet is also an accumulation of notes that address possible treatment and intervention recommendations. The ones drawn from the text boxes in Chapter 4 are based on the experience and judgments of the test authors. Other sources of possibilities should come from your own background in theory and supervised training experiences, certainly informed by ongoing empirical research. This section will likely transfer to your final report in the recommendations section rather than in the test results section.

The steps just described should result in a narrative report of findings that describes the client's personality and psychopathology not only in significant detail and with a high level of accuracy but also in a manner that is highly consistent with the report that would be produced any another appropriately trained clinical psychologist. As has been noted several times, the test interpretation approach advocated here is tightly aligned with the recommendations of the test authors. Reliability of test interpretation is very important for our field as a whole; the report on the MMPI–2–RF test results should be entirely based on the client's responses, not an individual psychologist's particular interpretation of those responses.

Conclusion

In this book, the recommendations for administration and scoring follow directly from the *Manual for Administration, Scoring, and Interpretation* (Ben-Porath & Tellegen, 2008/2011), as do the interpretive statements in the text boxes in Chapters 3 and 4. The interpretive framework here is the one explicated by Ben-Porath (2012b, Chapter 8), the senior author of the test. For students and new users of the MMPI–2–RF, following these stepwise procedures, including the use of the Interpretation Worksheet, is strongly recommended as a way to acquire expertise with the test as quickly as possible. Note as well, though, that the interpretive framework, the standard scale interpretations, and the use of the Interpretation Worksheet should be seen as standard practice, regardless of the experience level of the practitioner.

Case Example 6

In this chapter I present a case example that will provide a demonstration of the interpretive approach to the Minnesota Multiphasic Personality Inventory—2—Restructured Form (MMPI–2–RF) described in Chapter 5. A full Score Report is reproduced and discussed in light of the interpretive information presented in Chapters 3 and 4. I suggest that you have available an electronic version of the Interpretation Worksheet so that you can practice the method being described here and immediately compare your interpretations with the examples given.

Background

Jane C. Doe is a 21-year-old female college student. She completed a 2-year associate's degree at her local community college and transferred to a medium-sized regional comprehensive university. She is now a senior and is considering graduate school. Jane's grades are generally satisfactory, but she reports a history of a reading disability, and she received special education services for both reading and writing when she was in elementary school. She requested a full psychological evaluation in order to identify any current or residual learning problems; pending results, she may request accommodations on the upcoming Graduate Record Exam.

http://dx.doi.org/10.1037/0000074-007
Assessment Using the MMPI–2–RF, by D. M. McCord

Jane's MMPI–2–RF Score Report is reproduced in Figure 6.1, and the completed Interpretation Worksheet is included in Figure 6.2. As a reminder, you will use the scores-by-domain summary sheet of the Score Report (page 7 of Figure 6.1) to transfer scores to the Interpretation Worksheet during the second pass of the interpretation process. Also, note that the actual text of items listed on page 8 of the Score Report, "Item-Level Information," has been redacted in this reproduction as required by the copyright holder but would normally be visible on the report.

First Pass

The first pass is your overall orientation to the case. It is useful to consider the basic contextual information, presented here in the first paragraph of this chapter. Then simply page through the five graphic profile sheets of MMPI–2–RF data: (1) Protocol Validity Scales; (2) Higher-Order and Restructured Clinical (RC) Scales; (3) Specific Problems (SP) Scales for the Somatic/Cognitive and Internalizing domains; (4) SP Scales for the Externalizing and Interpersonal Functioning domains, plus the two Interest Scales; and (5) the Personality Psychopathology Five (PSY–5) Scales. This overview should take no more than 5 minutes. On all graphs, three hyphens mark the highest and lowest possible *T* score for each scale. Also, the profile sheet for the Protocol Validity Scales (page 2) does not include a horizontal line at $T = 65$, the cut point for clinical elevation on all other scales; this is because the interpretations for scores on the validity scales differ significantly, and the line at 65 is not meaningful.

PROTOCOL VALIDITY SCALES

Briefly consider the four broad questions addressed by the Protocol Validity indicators (page 2 of Figure 6.1). Was the test taker responsive, answering all items? In Jane's case, you can see (from Cannot Say *[CNS]* = 1) that one item was omitted, so overall she was responsive. However, you would make a mental note to follow up on this item, as a single omission from some of the brief scales can impact the accuracy of the scale. Second, was the test taker consistent in responding? Variable Response Inconsistency *(VRIN-r)* and True Response Inconsistency *(TRIN-r)* are very close to the general population means and within normal limits of the comparison group, so you would view Jane as being very consistent in her approach to the items.

Next, is there evidence of a tendency to overreport psychopathology? The five validity scales addressing this issue (Infrequent Responses *[F-r]*, Infrequent Psychopathology Responses *[Fp-r]*, Infrequent Somatic Responses *[Fs]*, Symptom Validity *[FBS-r]*, and Response Bias Scale *[RBS]*) have scores well within normal limits. Similarly, with regard to the final question concerning a tendency to underreport psychopathology, both Uncommon Virtues *(L-r)* and Adjustment Validity *(K-r)* are below the cutoffs. Overall, you see no threats to the validity of this protocol.

FIGURE 6.1

Minnesota Multiphasic
Personality Inventory-2
Restructured Form®

Score Report

MMPI-2-RF®
Minnesota Multiphasic Personality Inventory-2-Restructured Form®
Yossef S. Ben-Porath, PhD, & Auke Tellegen, PhD

Name:	Jane C. Doe
ID Number:	2015004
Age:	21
Gender:	Female
Marital Status:	Never Married
Years of Education:	Not reported
Date Assessed:	01/30/2015

(*continues*)

FIGURE 6.1 (*Continued*)

MMPI-2-RF® Score Report
01/30/2015, Page 2

ID: 2015004
Jane C. Doe

MMPI-2-RF Validity Scales

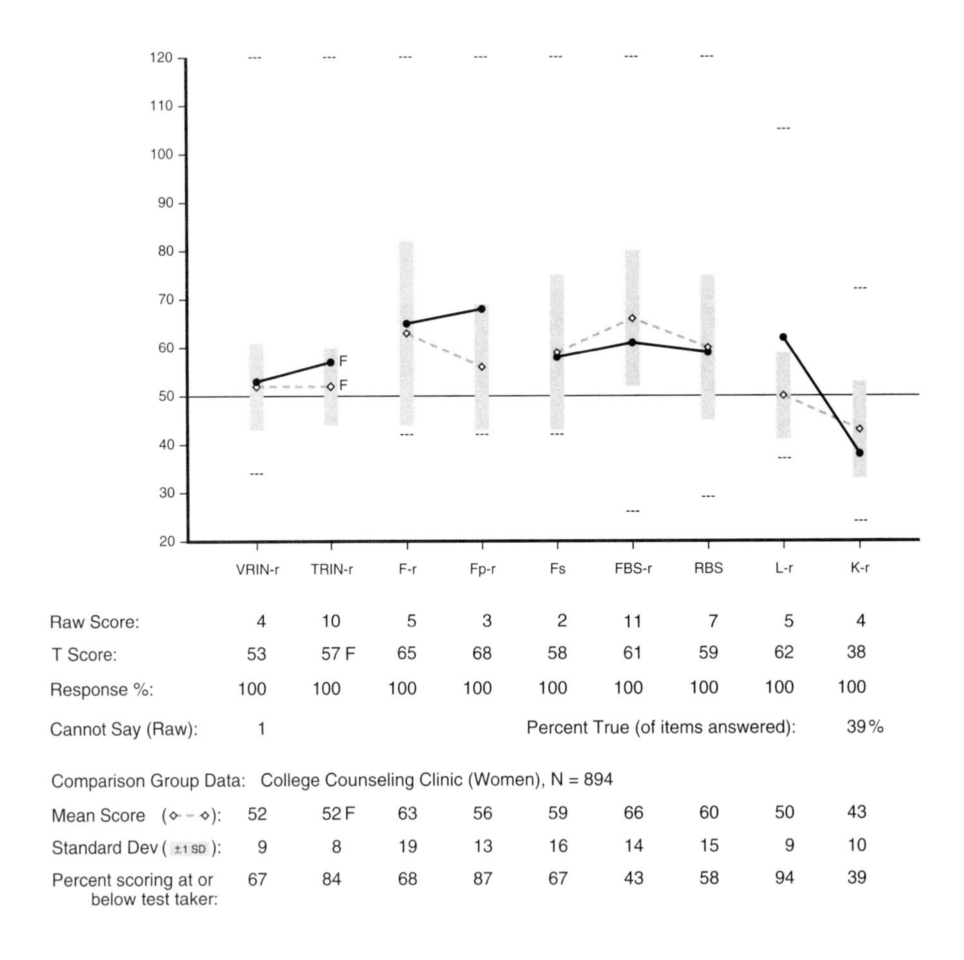

	VRIN-r	TRIN-r	F-r	Fp-r	Fs	FBS-r	RBS	L-r	K-r
Raw Score:	4	10	5	3	2	11	7	5	4
T Score:	53	57 F	65	68	58	61	59	62	38
Response %:	100	100	100	100	100	100	100	100	100

Cannot Say (Raw): 1 Percent True (of items answered): 39%

Comparison Group Data: College Counseling Clinic (Women), N = 894

	VRIN-r	TRIN-r	F-r	Fp-r	Fs	FBS-r	RBS	L-r	K-r
Mean Score (◇- - ◇):	52	52 F	63	56	59	66	60	50	43
Standard Dev (±1 SD):	9	8	19	13	16	14	15	9	10
Percent scoring at or below test taker:	67	84	68	87	67	43	58	94	39

The highest and lowest T scores possible on each scale are indicated by a "---"; MMPI-2-RF T scores are non-gendered.

VRIN-r Variable Response Inconsistency
TRIN-r True Response Inconsistency
F-r Infrequent Responses
Fp-r Infrequent Psychopathology Responses
Fs Infrequent Somatic Responses
FBS-r Symptom Validity
RBS Response Bias Scale
L-r Uncommon Virtues
K-r Adjustment Validity

FIGURE 6.1 (*Continued*)

MMPI-2-RF® Score Report
01/30/2015, Page 3

ID: 2015004
Jane C. Doe

MMPI-2-RF Higher-Order (H-O) and Restructured Clinical (RC) Scales

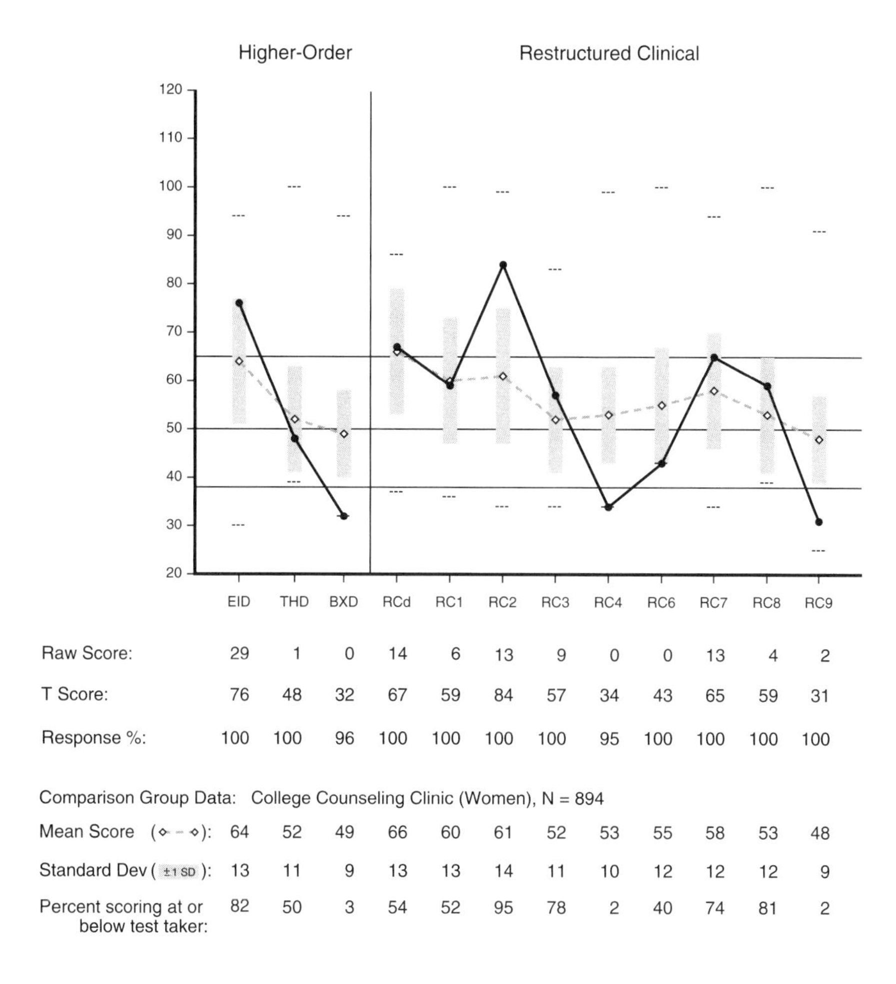

	EID	THD	BXD	RCd	RC1	RC2	RC3	RC4	RC6	RC7	RC8	RC9
Raw Score:	29	1	0	14	6	13	9	0	0	13	4	2
T Score:	76	48	32	67	59	84	57	34	43	65	59	31
Response %:	100	100	96	100	100	100	100	95	100	100	100	100

Comparison Group Data: College Counseling Clinic (Women), N = 894

	EID	THD	BXD	RCd	RC1	RC2	RC3	RC4	RC6	RC7	RC8	RC9
Mean Score (◇- - ◇):	64	52	49	66	60	61	52	53	55	58	53	48
Standard Dev (±1 SD):	13	11	9	13	13	14	11	10	12	12	12	9
Percent scoring at or below test taker:	82	50	3	54	52	95	78	2	40	74	81	2

The highest and lowest T scores possible on each scale are indicated by a "---"; MMPI-2-RF T scores are non-gendered.

EID Emotional/Internalizing Dysfunction
THD Thought Dysfunction
BXD Behavioral/Externalizing Dysfunction

RCd Demoralization
RC1 Somatic Complaints
RC2 Low Positive Emotions
RC3 Cynicism
RC4 Antisocial Behavior

RC6 Ideas of Persecution
RC7 Dysfunctional Negative Emotions
RC8 Aberrant Experiences
RC9 Hypomanic Activation

(*continues*)

FIGURE 6.1 (*Continued*)

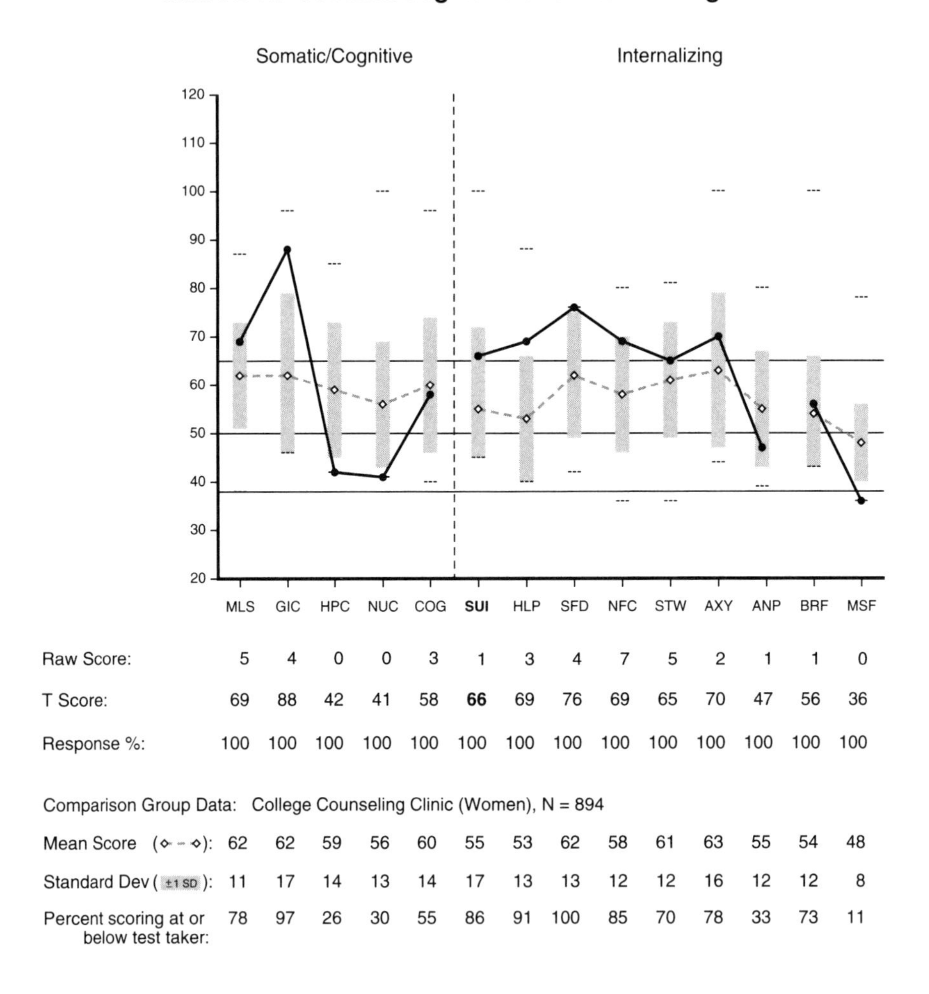

	MLS	GIC	HPC	NUC	COG	**SUI**	HLP	SFD	NFC	STW	AXY	ANP	BRF	MSF
Raw Score:	5	4	0	0	3	1	3	4	7	5	2	1	1	0
T Score:	69	88	42	41	58	**66**	69	76	69	65	70	47	56	36
Response %:	100	100	100	100	100	100	100	100	100	100	100	100	100	100

Comparison Group Data: College Counseling Clinic (Women), N = 894

Mean Score (◇- -◇):	62	62	59	56	60	55	53	62	58	61	63	55	54	48
Standard Dev (±1 SD):	11	17	14	13	14	17	13	13	12	12	16	12	12	8
Percent scoring at or below test taker:	78	97	26	30	55	86	91	100	85	70	78	33	73	11

The highest and lowest T scores possible on each scale are indicated by a "---"; MMPI-2-RF T scores are non-gendered.

MLS	Malaise	SUI	Suicidal/Death Ideation	AXY	Anxiety
GIC	Gastrointestinal Complaints	HLP	Helplessness/Hopelessness	ANP	Anger Proneness
HPC	Head Pain Complaints	SFD	Self-Doubt	BRF	Behavior-Restricting Fears
NUC	Neurological Complaints	NFC	Inefficacy	MSF	Multiple Specific Fears
COG	Cognitive Complaints	STW	Stress/Worry		

FIGURE 6.1 (*Continued*)

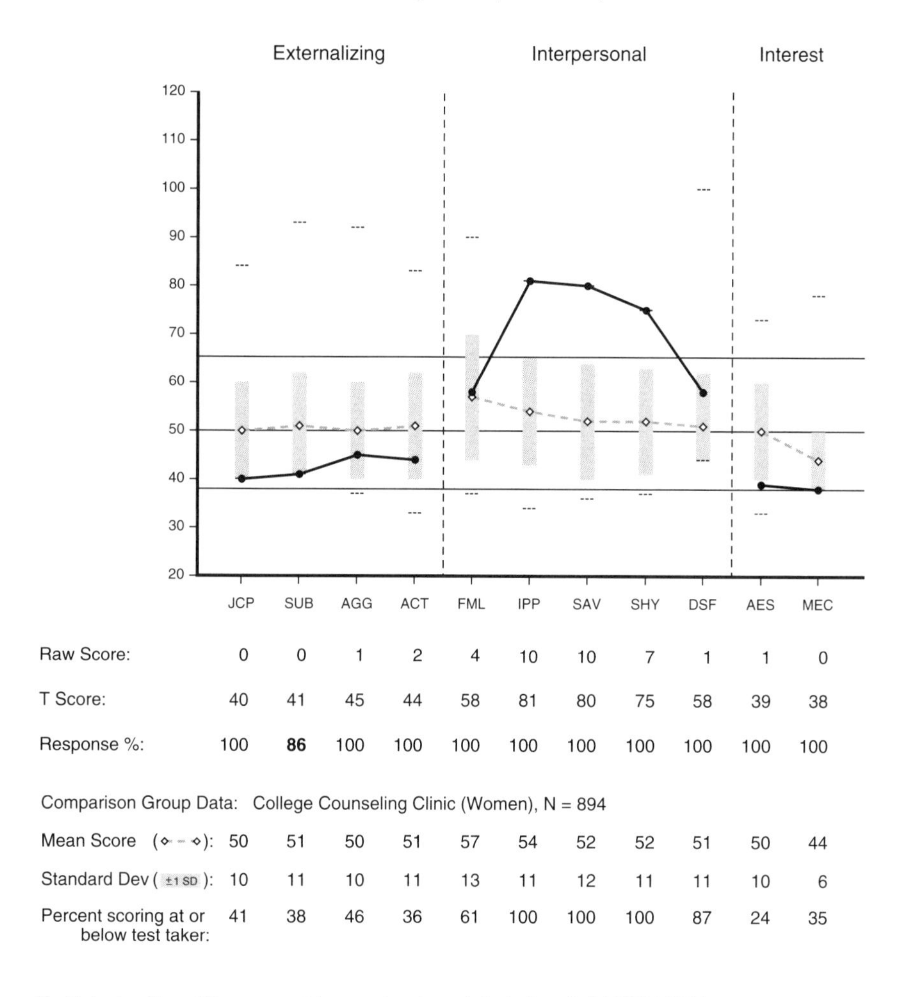

	JCP	SUB	AGG	ACT	FML	IPP	SAV	SHY	DSF	AES	MEC
Raw Score:	0	0	1	2	4	10	10	7	1	1	0
T Score:	40	41	45	44	58	81	80	75	58	39	38
Response %:	100	**86**	100	100	100	100	100	100	100	100	100

Comparison Group Data: College Counseling Clinic (Women), N = 894

	JCP	SUB	AGG	ACT	FML	IPP	SAV	SHY	DSF	AES	MEC
Mean Score (◇- -◇):	50	51	50	51	57	54	52	52	51	50	44
Standard Dev (±1 SD):	10	11	10	11	13	11	12	11	11	10	6
Percent scoring at or below test taker:	41	38	46	36	61	100	100	100	87	24	35

The highest and lowest T scores possible on each scale are indicated by a "---"; MMPI-2-RF T scores are non-gendered.

JCP Juvenile Conduct Problems
SUB Substance Abuse
AGG Aggression
ACT Activation

FML Family Problems
IPP Interpersonal Passivity
SAV Social Avoidance
SHY Shyness
DSF Disaffiliativeness

AES Aesthetic-Literary Interests
MEC Mechanical-Physical Interests

(*continues*)

FIGURE 6.1 (*Continued*)

MMPI-2-RF® Score Report
01/30/2015, Page 6

ID: 2015004
Jane C. Doe

MMPI-2-RF PSY-5 Scales

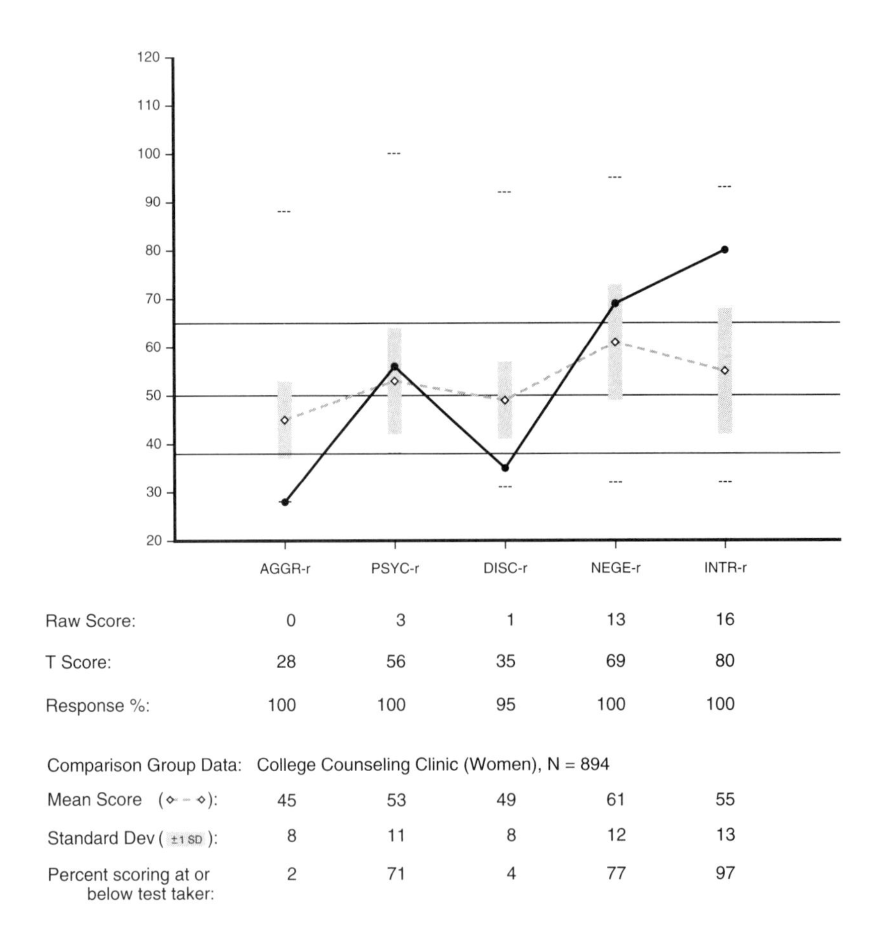

	AGGR-r	PSYC-r	DISC-r	NEGE-r	INTR-r
Raw Score:	0	3	1	13	16
T Score:	28	56	35	69	80
Response %:	100	100	95	100	100

Comparison Group Data: College Counseling Clinic (Women), N = 894

	AGGR-r	PSYC-r	DISC-r	NEGE-r	INTR-r
Mean Score (◇- - ◇):	45	53	49	61	55
Standard Dev (±1 SD):	8	11	8	12	13
Percent scoring at or below test taker:	2	71	4	77	97

The highest and lowest T scores possible on each scale are indicated by a "---"; MMPI-2-RF T scores are non-gendered.

AGGR-r Aggressiveness-Revised
PSYC-r Psychoticism-Revised
DISC-r Disconstraint-Revised
NEGE-r Negative Emotionality/Neuroticism-Revised
INTR-r Introversion/Low Positive Emotionality-Revised

FIGURE 6.1 (*Continued*)

MMPI-2-RF® Score Report
01/30/2015, Page 7

ID: 2015004
Jane C. Doe

MMPI-2-RF T SCORES (BY DOMAIN)

PROTOCOL VALIDITY

Domain	Higher-Order	Scale scores						
Content Non-Responsiveness		1 CNS	53 VRIN-r	57 F TRIN-r				
Over-Reporting		65 F-r	68 Fp-r		58 Fs	61 FBS-r	59 RBS	
Under-Reporting		62 L-r	38 K-r					

SUBSTANTIVE SCALES

Domain	Higher-Order	Scale scores						
Somatic/Cognitive Dysfunction		59 RC1	69 MLS	88 GIC	42 HPC	41 NUC	58 COG	
Emotional Dysfunction	76 EID	67 RCd	66 SUI	69 HLP	76 SFD	69 NFC		
		84 RC2	80 INTR-r					
		65 RC7	65 STW	70 AXY	47 ANP	56 BRF	36 MSF	69 NEGE-r
Thought Dysfunction	48 THD	43 RC6						
		59 RC8						
		56 PSYC-r						
Behavioral Dysfunction	32 BXD	34 RC4	40 JCP	41* SUB				
		31 RC9	45 AGG	44 ACT	28 AGGR-r	35 DISC-r		
Interpersonal Functioning		58 FML	57 RC3	81 IPP	80 SAV	75 SHY	58 DSF	
Interests		39 AES	38 MEC					

*The test taker provided scorable responses to less than 90% of the items scored on this scale. See the relevant profile page for the specific percentage.

Note. This information is provided to facilitate interpretation following the recommended structure for MMPI-2-RF interpretation in Chapter 5 of the *MMPI-2-RF Manual for Administration, Scoring, and Interpretation*, which provides details in the text and an outline in Table 5-1.

(*continues*)

FIGURE 6.1 (*Continued*)

MMPI-2-RF® Score Report
01/30/2015, Page 8

ID: 2015004
Jane C. Doe

ITEM-LEVEL INFORMATION

Unscorable Responses

Following is a list of items to which the test taker did not provide scorable responses. Unanswered or double answered (both True and False) items are unscorable. The scales on which the items appear are in parentheses following the item content.

49. [redacted]. (BXD, RC4, SUB, DISC-r)

Critical Responses

Seven MMPI-2-RF scales--Suicidal/Death Ideation (SUI), Helplessness/Hopelessness (HLP), Anxiety (AXY), Ideas of Persecution (RC6), Aberrant Experiences (RC8), Substance Abuse (SUB), and Aggression (AGG)--have been designated by the test authors as having critical item content that may require immediate attention and follow-up. Items answered by the individual in the keyed direction (True or False) on a critical scale are listed below if her T score on that scale is 65 or higher. The percentage of the MMPI-2-RF normative sample (NS) and of the College Counseling Clinic (Women) comparison group (CG) that answered each item in the keyed direction are provided in parentheses following the item content.

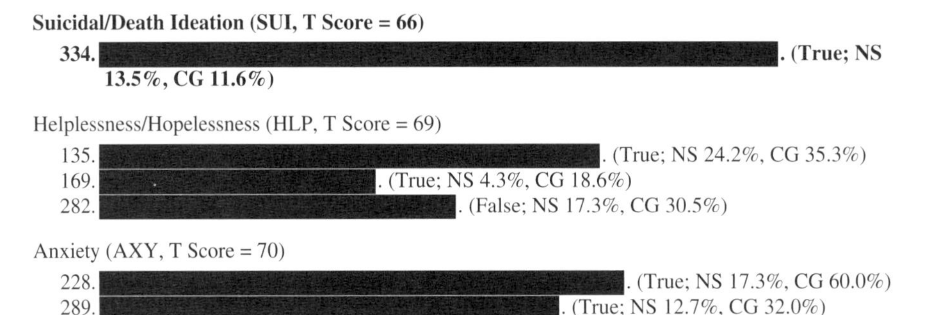

Suicidal/Death Ideation (SUI, T Score = 66)

334. [redacted]. (True; NS 13.5%, CG 11.6%)

Helplessness/Hopelessness (HLP, T Score = 69)

135. [redacted]. (True; NS 24.2%, CG 35.3%)
169. [redacted]. (True; NS 4.3%, CG 18.6%)
282. [redacted]. (False; NS 17.3%, CG 30.5%)

Anxiety (AXY, T Score = 70)

228. [redacted]. (True; NS 17.3%, CG 60.0%)
289. [redacted]. (True; NS 12.7%, CG 32.0%)

User-Designated Item-Level Information

The following item-level information is based on the report user's selection of additional scales, and/or of lower cutoffs for the critical scales from the previous section. Items answered by the test taker in the keyed direction (True or False) on a selected scale are listed below if her T score on that scale is at the user-designated cutoff score or higher.

The test taker has not produced an elevated T score (based on user-designated cutoffs) on any of the selected scales.

End of Report

Score report. Reproduced with permission by the University of Minnesota Press.

FIGURE 6.2

MMPI-2-RF® Interpretation Worksheet

Protocol Validity

Content Non-Responsiveness CNS 1 VRIN-r 53 TRIN-r 57F

The test-taker omitted only 1 of the 338 items, reflecting an acceptable level of responsiveness overall. SUB Response % is 86.

There are no indications of inconsistent responding.

Over-Reporting F-r 65 Fp-r 68 Fs 58 FBS-r 61 RBS 59

There are no indications of overreporting.

Under-Reporting L-r 62 K-r 38

There are no indications of underreporting.

(continues)

FIGURE 6.2 (*Continued*)

Substantive Scale Interpretation

Somatic/Cognitive Dysfunction RC1 59 GIC 88 NUC 41

MLS 69 HPC 42 COG 58

The client reports a number of gastrointestinal complaints. She also reports experiencing poor health and feeling weak or tired.

Emotional Dysfunction EID 76 RCd 67 RC2 84 RC7 65

SUI 66 INTR-r 80 STW 65

HLP 69 AXY 70

SFD 76 ANP 47

NFC 69 BRF 56

MSF 36

NEGE-r 69

Ms. Doe's responses to the MMPI-2-RF indicate significant emotional distress. She reports significant anhedonia, characterized by a lack of positive emotional experiences in her life and a lack of interests. She reports feeling sad and unhappy, and being very dissatisfied with her current life circumstances. Ms. Doe reports lacking confidence and feeling useless. She also reports feeling hopeless and pessimistic. Other people with similar elevations feel overwhelmed and that life is a strain, and they believe that they cannot be helped. Further, Ms. Doe reports being passive, indecisive, and inefficacious, and she believes that she is not capable of dealing with her current difficulties. Of particular and immediate concern is Ms. Doe's acknowledgment of a history of suicidal ideation and attempts. She may be preoccupied with thoughts of suicide and death. Risk for suicide must be immediately addressed. Additionally, Ms. Doe reports various other negative emotional experiences, including anxiety and fear. She is likely to experience intense anxiety and anxiety related problems, including intrusive ideation, sleep difficulties, nightmares, and post-traumatic distress. She reports an above-average level of stress and worry, and it is likely that she is stress-reactive and worry-prone, with a tendency to engage in obsessive rumination.

FIGURE 6.2 (*Continued*)

Thought Dysfunction THD 48 RC6 43 RC8 59 PSYC-r 56

There are no indications of thought dysfunction.

Behavioral Dysfunction BXD 32 RC4 34 RC9 31 AGGR-r 28

JCP 40 AGG 45 DISC-r 35

SUB 41 ACT 44

Ms. Doe's responses indicate a higher than average level of behavioral constraint; she is unlikely to engage in externalizing, acting-out behavior. She reports a below-average level of past antisocial behavior. She reports a below-average level of activation and engagement with her environment. It is likely that she has a low energy level and is disengaged from her environment.

She reports being interpersonally passive and submissive.
She reports overly constrained behavior.

Interpersonal Functioning: FML 58 RC3 57 IPP 81 SAV 80 SHY 75 DSF 58

Ms. Doe reports being unassertive and submissive, and that she is not likely to be in charge of tasks or situations. She fails to stand up for herself and is ready to give in to others. It is likely that her passivity and submissiveness are evident in interpersonal relationships. Ms. Doe reports not enjoying social events and avoiding social situations. She likely has difficulty forming close relationships, is introverted, and is emotionally restricted. She reports being shy, easily embarrassed, and uncomfortable around others. As noted earlier, she is generally very anxious, and this is likely to be particularly true in social situations.

Interests: AES 39 MEC 38

She reports no interest in activities or occupations of an aesthetic or literary nature (e.g., writing, music, the theater), nor does she report interest in activities or occupations of a mechanical or physical nature (e.g., fixing and building things, the outdoors, sports).

(*continues*)

FIGURE 6.2 (*Continued*)

Diagnostic Considerations

Consider somatoform disorder if physical cause of elevated GIC and MLS has been ruled out.
Evaluate for internalizing disorders. Suicidality is an immediate concern.
Evaluate for depressive disorder, including major depression.
Evaluate for disorders characterized by passive-submissive behavior such as dependent personality disorder.
Evaluate for disorders associated with social avoidance such as avoidant personality disorder.

Treatment Considerations

Malaise may reduce engagement and motivation for treatment.
Recommend physical evaluation of both malaise and gastrointestinal complaints.
If gastrointestinal symptoms appear to be stress related, consider stress reduction approaches.
Emotional distress may motivate her for treatment.
Reduction of emotional distress should be considered as an initial target for treatment.
Need for antidepressant medication should be considered.
Need for inpatient treatment should be evaluated.
Risk for suicide should be immediately addressed.
Low positive emotionality may interfere with engagement in treatment.
Anxiety is an appropriate target for treatment, as is her exclusive focus on negative information.
Reducing passive, submissive behavior is an appropriate target for intervention.
Difficulties associated with social avoidance are appropriate targets for intervention.

HIGHER-ORDER AND RESTRUCTURED CLINICAL SCALES

Focus first on the three Higher-Order Scales, as they provide a very important perspective on prioritizing the findings (page 3 of Figure 6.1). Jane has produced a clinically elevated score on Emotional/Internalizing Dysfunction *(EID)*, a normal-range score on Thought Dysfunction *(THD)*, and the lowest score possible on Behavioral/Externalizing Dysfunction *(BXD)*. Thus, you can tell from the outset that your focus will be on the Internalizing domain. This initial impression is clearly corroborated by the pattern of RC Scale elevations Jane produced: Demoralization *(RCd)*, Low Positive Emotions *(RC2)*, and Dysfunctional Negative Emotions *(RC7)*. You would also note that Antisocial Behavior *(RC4)* and Hypomanic Activation *(RC9)* are both notably low. It is also interesting that among the three midlevel constructs associated with *EID*, *RC2* is clearly higher than the other two, suggesting a level of depressivity that may be clinically relevant.

SPECIFIC PROBLEMS AND INTEREST SCALES

The 23 SP Scales provide the most specific level of measurement (pages 4 and 5 of Figure 6.1). These scores are organized by domain. As you scan these profile sheets in your first pass, make note of any clinical elevations as well as notably low scores. In Jane's case, you would anticipate elevations among the Internalizing SP Scales. It is important to remember, though, that clinical elevations on the SP Scales in any domain are interpretable by themselves, even if the higher level scales in that domain were not elevated. For example, Jane's Gastrointestinal Complaints *(GIC)* score is high enough to indicate frequent complaints of gastrointestinal problems, despite the fact that Somatic Complaints *(RC1)* is not itself elevated.

All four facets of *RCd* are elevated: Suicidal/Death Ideation *(SUI)*, Helplessness/Hopelessness *(HLP)*, Self-Doubt *(SFD)*, and Inefficacy *(NFC)*. You see that *SUI* is bolded to draw your attention. One item was endorsed. You know that this item will be printed on page 8 of the Score Report, the item-level information section, and clearly follow-up questioning is warranted prior to Jane's departure from the assessment session. Stress/Worry *(STW)* and Anxiety *(AXY)* are also clinically elevated.

Not surprisingly, all SP Scales in the Externalizing domain are very low, consistent with all other data thus far. A number of substantial elevations occur among the SP Scales in the Interpersonal Functioning domain, including Interpersonal Passivity *(IPP)*, Social Avoidance *(SAV)*, and Shyness *(SHY)*.

PSY–5 SCALES

The last profile sheet presents the PSY–5 data (page 6 of Figure 6.1). In your second pass, you place these constructs in the narrow level of the domain with which they are associated, and they may or may not provide additional narrative interpretation by the time they are considered. In the first pass, these constructs are best seen as broad factors of personality and psychopathology that can provide another angle on your pattern of data. In Jane's case, you see two clinically elevated scales, Negative

Emotionality/Neuroticism–Revised *(NEGE-r)* and Introversion/Low Positive Emotionality *(INTR-r)*, both quite consistent with other data. The fact that *INTR-r* is clearly the highest scale supports your earlier impression that depression may well be a significant factor in this case. We will skip page 7 of the Score Report for now and return to it in the second pass.

ITEM-LEVEL INFORMATION

On the item-level information sheet (page 8 of Figure 6.1), you see the text of the one item that Jane omitted and note that she scored above the cut point on three of the seven scales designated as having critical content (*SUI, HLP*, and *AXY*). The item she omitted concerned the use of marijuana, and you can see that it is scored on Behavioral/Externalizing Dysfunction *(BXD)*, Antisocial Behavior *(RC4)*, Substance Abuse *(SUB)*, and Disconstraint–Revised *(DISC-r)*. You check the profile graph on page 5 of the Score Report to see that Response % for *SUB* is 86%, an issue to consider in interpretation. You see the text of the one *SUI* item endorsed, and, as noted above, this will certainly trigger immediate assessment of suicidality. The *HLP* items can be clarified in follow-up interview as well. One of the two endorsed *AXY* items refers to general anxiety, which is not an infrequent response, and the other refers to frightening dreams, which is relatively rarely endorsed. Again, these responses can provide prompts for follow-up interview.

So, at the end of your brief first pass, you are able to obtain a clear picture of Jane's pattern of psychological difficulty, and you have a generally clear plan of attack. The Internalizing domain dominates this picture, with clinically relevant elevations on all three midlevel factors. The order of the RC Scale scores in this domain (*RC2* > *RCd* > *RC7*) is corroborated by the high *INTR-r* score among the PSY–5 Scales, strongly suggesting that your report will move from the overall *EID* level to the depressivity data *(RC2)*, followed by distress/demoralization *(RCd)*, including the suicidal thoughts, and then move to the anxiety symptoms *(RC7)*. The notably high *GIC* score may be included in the context of these internalizing issues. The Interpersonal Functioning issues will then follow.

Second Pass

As described in Chapter 5, the second pass requires that you have two items available. First, have a handy version of page 7 of the Score Report (Figure 6.1), the scores-by-domain summary sheet. Second, you need a blank version of the Interpretation Worksheet (Figure 6.2). In addition, because you used a comparison group in this case (the College Counseling Clinic sample), you will need to refer at times to the profile sheets, as the comparison group information is not included in the scores-by-domain summary. The first step is to transfer the 52 scores (*CNS* count plus 51 scale scores) from the scores-by-domain report page to the appropriate blanks in the four-page Interpretation Worksheet. You then apply the steps described in Chapter 5 to complete the worksheet. The worksheet itself is presented here, and the narrative sections that follow provide a commentary on the process.

PROTOCOL VALIDITY SCALES

The Interpretation Worksheet guides you through the considerations of responsiveness, consistency, overreporting, and underreporting, which you will report on page 1 of the Interpretation Worksheet. As you noted in the first pass, *CNS* = 1. The omission of even a single item requires some interpretive consideration on your part, as this omission could reduce the response rate below 90% on some of the shorter scales on the MMPI–2–RF. The quickest way to check this is to view the item-level information on page 8; the first section of this page deals with unscorable responses. You already did this on the first pass, as is recommended, and found that the single omitted item dealt with marijuana use and was scored on *BXD, RC4, SUB*, and *DISC-r*. Now check the graphs for these scales to find Response %. The single omission does not have any impact on your overall results other than *SUB*, for which it lowers the response rate to 86% (which is bolded to draw attention). Given the overall pattern of strikingly low scores on virtually all Externalizing Scales, this is not likely to reflect a problem of any sort. You may want to mark it for possible follow-up questioning on next contact with the client, but you can conclude that she was acceptably responsive and include this information on the worksheet. All other Protocol Validity indicators are well within normal limits, including relative to the comparison group, so you note on the worksheet that there were no indications of inconsistency, overreporting, or underreporting.

SOMATIC/COGNITIVE SCALES

There is no elevation on *RC1*, so no general overview statement is indicated in the Somatic/Cognitive Dysfunction section of page 2 of the Interpretation Worksheet. You would note that elevations occurred on two of the other five scales, *MLS* and *GIC*, and add content-based statements to the worksheet. In addition, you would add a diagnostic consideration regarding *GIC* and also several treatment-related comments to the appropriate sections on page 4 of the worksheet.

INTERNALIZING SCALES

As was evident in your first pass, Internalizing is the domain of primary interest and will lead off your ultimate narrative report (after addressing protocol validity, as always). Jane's *EID* score is 76, and you would add the appropriate content-based statement to the Emotional Dysfunction section on page 2 of the worksheet. You also would add the one diagnostic consideration and the one treatment consideration to page 4 of the worksheet. Although there are numerous empirical correlates of *EID*, you can see at a glance that these are concepts addressed by the lower level scales that themselves are elevated in this profile. Your report will be more coherent and less repetitive if you address these issues on the worksheet in the context of the lower level scales.

All three midlevel scales are elevated in this domain, and *RC2* is clearly the highest. Thus, the second sentence of your narrative in the Emotional Dysfunction section would combine the content elements associated with this elevation ($T = 84$). The next scale to consider is *INTR-r*, and the first content-based statement (lack of positive emotional experiences) has already been covered. The second content element has to do with avoidance of social situations. A quick glance at the Interpersonal Functioning Scales you scanned in your first pass reminds you that there were significant elevations on several related measures, so it is reasonable to skip this element for now, knowing that you will address this important issue later in the context of interpersonal functioning (page 3 of the worksheet).

The next midlevel scale by elevation is *RCd*, and you can see that all of its facet scales are also elevated. You would add elevation-determined content-based statements for *RCd* and then for the facet scales to the worksheet, in descending order of elevation. Examination of the correlates for *RCd* indicates that most of the elements are also covered in the facet scales. You would give particular emphasis to the elevated *SUI* scale, of course, and you would include the need for an immediate risk assessment both in the narrative paragraph and in the treatment considerations. Finally, the *RC7* strand, which includes *AXY*, *NEGE-r*, and *STW*, adds new elements of anxiety, fears, and obsessive rumination. You would blend content-based statements with correlate-based statements with the goal of including all relevant elements while avoiding redundancy. As noted earlier, your Emotional Dysfunction paragraph should be amenable to direct cut and paste into the final report, as will be seen below.

THOUGHT DYSFUNCTION SCALES

THD is not elevated at all, nor are Ideas of Persecution *(RC6)*, Aberrant Experiences *(RC8)*, or Psychoticism–Revised *(PSYC-r)*. Thus, one simple statement suffices in the Thought Dysfunction section on page 3 of the worksheet, and no information needs to be transferred to the final report.

EXTERNALIZING SCALES

Jane has no elevated scores in the Externalizing domain. However, several of the scales in this domain have content-based interpretive statements as well as empirical correlates associated with very low scores. Thus, you would add statements for low scores on Behavioral/Externalizing Dysfunction *(BXD)*, Antisocial Behavior *(RC4)*, and Hypomanic Activation *(RC9)* to the Behavioral Dysfunction section on page 3 of the worksheet. Similarly, you would add low-score interpretive statements for Aggressiveness–Revised *(AGGR-r)* and Disconstraint–Revised *(DISC-r)*, although these elements are redundant and would not be transferred to the final psychological report in this case.

INTERPERSONAL FUNCTIONING SCALES

Remember that there is no hierarchical order for the Interpersonal Functioning Scales, so you would interpret each of these six scales independently, in descending order by scale elevation, in the Interpersonal Functioning section on page 3 of the Interpretation Worksheet. In this case, you see elevations in *IPP, SAV,* and *SHY,* in that order. From the text boxes in Chapter 4, you would add the content-based statements to the worksheet, as well as nonredundant empirical correlates. You may make some effort to integrate this paragraph into the context of the final report by referring to an earlier finding, which may facilitate the transfer of the narrative on the worksheet to your final psychological report.

INTEREST SCALES

Although these two residual scales have been deemphasized in this practical guidebook, the present case is a clear example in which they are useful. Based on significant elevations of *RC2* and *INTR-r* in a valid protocol, you could advance the interpretation that anhedonia, lack of positive emotions, and lack of environmental engagement are key features of the case in the Interests section on page 3 of the worksheet. These very low scores on Interest Scales reflecting both of the broad categories of activities and occupations are consistent with the clinical findings and add an element of real-life relevance to the test results.

DIAGNOSTIC CONSIDERATIONS

The comments and recommendations in the Diagnostic Considerations section of the Interpretation Worksheet (page 4) echo those included in the *Manual for Administration, Scoring, and Interpretation* (Ben-Porath & Tellegen, 2008/2011). Given the major paradigm shift described in Chapter 1, it may seem odd that your notations in this section would refer to traditional diagnostic categories and syndromes. Even so, present reality often requires some degree of alignment with the major diagnostic coding in the field (the fifth edition of the *Diagnostic and Statistical Manual of Mental Disorders* [American Psychiatric Association, 2013] and the 10th revision of the *International Classification of Diseases* [World Health Organization, 1992], at the time of this writing), and it is helpful to offer some pointers to these systems as you go through the data. Bear in mind, though, that in the present case, your thorough description of the characteristics associated with Jane's elevations on this relatively comprehensive set of dimensional constructs is far more informative than the label of major depressive disorder or avoidant personality disorder.

TREATMENT CONSIDERATIONS

The Treatment Considerations section of the worksheet (page 4) will be particularly helpful in the preparation of your final psychological report. For the most part, these recommendations for intervention are based on the judgment and experience of the test authors. Like the interpretive information in the text boxes in Chapters 3 and 4, these treatment recommendations reflect either a high level of face validity (e.g., if stress levels are high, stress reduction therapeutic techniques are recommended) or well-established empirical findings (e.g., if *RC2* is elevated, both cognitive–behavioral therapy and antidepressant medication should be considered).

Preparation of the Final Narrative Report

Generally speaking, most narrative psychological reports have a section on test results, and then following the description of all test results in the battery, a concluding section integrates findings, offers diagnostic formulations if needed, and makes recommendations for intervention. As you integrate MMPI–2–RF data into the final report, using the Interpretation Worksheet as your source, you will often cut and paste the first four sections in order of salience for the specific case, and then the Interpersonal Functioning section. You would include diagnostic suggestions and treatment recommendations in a more customized manner, considering the role of other data in the context of the specific case.

In the test results section, after transferring the four primary paragraphs, it is important to go back through these and add introductory, transition, or summary statements as warranted. In the case example, the order of primary paragraphs will be Emotional Dysfunction, Somatic/Cognitive Dysfunction, and Behavioral Dysfunction (with low score interpretations). You would not have a separate paragraph for Thought Dysfunction, but you would note in the report that there was no evidence of problems in this area with a single statement at the end of the Behavioral Dysfunction paragraph. You would then add the Interpersonal Functioning paragraph, which will conclude the MMPI–2–RF results.

For illustrative purposes, you would add a paragraph with treatment considerations, although, as noted above, in many psychological reporting formats this information would be incorporated in a concluding section of the report and integrated with other data. Exhibit 6.1 provides an example of how you could transfer interpretations for this case example from the worksheet to the full narrative report. Note that about 75% of this relatively lengthy narrative was cut and pasted directly from the Interpretation Worksheet. The primary work was done during the second pass of the interpretation process by extracting appropriate interpretive statements from the text boxes in Chapter 4 and typing them into the worksheet. As I have demonstrated here, it is not difficult to construct the primary paragraphs in the five key domains of the worksheet in coherent narrative form, greatly facilitating the process of transferring information from the worksheet to the final report.

Conclusion

In summary, I hope that this case example provides a clear example of the extraordinary usefulness of the MMPI–2–RF. Of the 40 psychopathology scales on the test, Jane produced clinical-range (or significantly low) scores on 23 of them. These results provide for a rich, detailed description of her as an individual, far more valuable than any categorical diagnostic label. In addition, the test approach described in this chapter also produces a relatively thorough treatment plan.

EXHIBIT 6.1

Example of a Full Narrative Report Composed by Transferring Interpretations From the Interpretation Worksheet

Ms. Doe completed the MMPI–2–RF, a broad-band measure of personality and psychopathology, as a component of the current evaluation. Validity indicators suggest that she read items carefully and responded in a consistent, thoughtful, systematic manner, neither overstating nor understating problems and issues in her life. This approach reflects a cooperative attitude, and the resulting profile is seen as an accurate reflection of her current psychological functioning.

Ms. Doe's responses to the MMPI–2–RF indicate significant emotional distress. She reports significant anhedonia, characterized by a lack of positive emotional experiences in her life and a lack of interests. She reports feeling sad and unhappy and being very dissatisfied with her current life circumstances. Ms. Doe reports lacking confidence and feeling useless. She also reports feeling hopeless and pessimistic. Other people with similar elevations feel overwhelmed and that life is a strain, and they believe that they cannot be helped. Further, Ms. Doe reports being passive, indecisive, and inefficacious, and she believes that she is not capable of dealing with her current difficulties.

Of particular and immediate concern is Ms. Doe's acknowledgment of a history of suicidal ideation and attempts. She may be preoccupied with thoughts of suicide and death. Risk for suicide must be immediately addressed. Additionally, Ms. Doe reports various other negative emotional experiences, including anxiety and fear. She is likely to experience intense anxiety and anxiety-related problems, including intrusive ideation, sleep difficulties, nightmares, and posttraumatic distress. She reports an above-average level of stress and worry, and it is likely that she is stress reactive and worry prone, with a tendency to engage in obsessive rumination. In addition, Ms. Doe reports a number of gastrointestinal complaints. She also reports experiencing poor health and feeling weak or tired.

Ms. Doe's responses indicate a higher-than-average level of behavioral constraint; she is unlikely to engage in externalizing, acting-out behavior. She reports a below-average level of past antisocial behavior. She similarly reports a below-average level of activation and engagement with her environment. It is likely that she has a low energy level and is disengaged from her environment.

Ms. Doe reports being unassertive and submissive, and she is not likely to be in charge of tasks or situations. She fails to stand up for herself and is ready to give in to others. It is likely that her passivity and submissiveness are evident in interpersonal relationships. Ms. Doe reports not enjoying social events and avoiding social situations. She likely has difficulty forming close relationships, is introverted, and is emotionally restricted. She reports being shy, easily embarrassed, and uncomfortable around others. As noted earlier, she is generally very anxious, and this is likely to be particularly true in social situations. She reports no interest in activities or occupations of an aesthetic or literary nature (e.g., writing, music, the theater), nor does she report interest in activities or occupations of a mechanical or physical nature (e.g., fixing and building things, the outdoors, sports). This pervasive lack of interests is consistent with the high levels of anhedonia and disengagement with her environment noted above.

Risk for suicide should be immediately assessed. Ms. Doe's high level of general emotional distress and unhappiness may provide some motivation for treatment, although her malaise may undermine this motivation, and low positive emotionality may interfere with therapeutic engagement. Both malaise and gastrointestinal complaints should be evaluated medically. Given the levels of depressive symptoms, including suicidal thoughts, the need for inpatient hospitalization should be considered, and antidepressant medication should also be considered. Initial targets for intervention include reduction of emotional distress and reduction of anxiety. Longer term goals should address her exclusive focus on negative information, her social avoidance, and her passive, submissive interpersonal behaviors.

Concluding Comments 7

The original Minnesota Multiphasic Personality Inventory (MMPI) was developed within an inpatient psychiatric setting, but it was soon incorporated into outpatient mental health settings, medical settings, and a variety of nonclinical settings (e.g., employment suitability screening for high-risk, high-impact occupations). The MMPI–2—Restructured Form (MMPI–2–RF) has been demonstrated empirically to be valid and useful in a wide range of settings as well, some of which are listed below.

With regard to general clinical settings, the Restructured Clinical Scales correlate well with target symptoms in psychiatric inpatients (Arbisi, Sellbom, & Ben-Porath, 2008) and outpatients (Tellegen & Ben-Porath, 2008/2011). Suicidal/Death Ideation *(SUI)* has been shown to be a remarkably sensitive and accurate scale (e.g., Gottfried, Bodell, Carbonell, & Joiner, 2014).

An extensive body of research has been conducted in various medical settings. The MMPI–2–RF has been demonstrated useful in the assessment of patients with chronic pain (e.g., McCord & Drerup, 2011), patients with seizure disorders (e.g., Myers, Fleming, Lancman, Perrine, & Lancman, 2013), and patients with other specific medical issues. Two areas generating significant empirical research are assessment of suitability and prediction of outcomes of spinal surgery (Block, Ben-Porath, & Marek, 2013) and of bariatric surgery (Marek, Block, & Ben-Porath, 2015).

http://dx.doi.org/10.1037/0000074-008
Assessment Using the MMPI–2–RF, by D. M. McCord

Another key specialty area for which the MMPI–2–RF is particularly well suited is forensic psychology, including parental assessment in child custody cases (e.g., Arce, Fariña, Seijo, & Novo, 2015), parental assessment in child abuse cases (e.g., Solomon, Morgan, Asberg, & McCord, 2014), validity of self-reporting in personal injury litigation (e.g., Sleep, Petty, & Wygant, 2015), aggression in forensic inpatients (e.g., Grossi et al., 2015), and assessment of disability claimants (Henry, Heilbronner, Mittenberg, Enders, & Domboski, 2009). Psychologists engaged in forensic practice are strongly advised to read and save the excellent articles by Ben-Porath (2012a) and Sellbom (2012) addressing key issues in this specialty area.

As noted in Chapter 2, a specific occupational category, police officer, has been a particular focus for MMPI–2–RF development. A specialized version of the Interpretive Report is available for this occupation, the Police Candidate Interpretive Report, and empirical research in this area is active (e.g., Tarescavage, Brewster, Corey, & Ben-Porath, 2015).

The perspective taken throughout most of this practical guide, reflected in the case example in Chapter 6, is that the MMPI–2–RF is administered as one component of a larger test battery, and the interpretations and recommendations are integrated into a comprehensive report. A comprehensive assessment typically includes a standardized battery of tests used to assess cognitive abilities and patterns; a separate battery of individually administered tests to measure academic achievement levels, strengths, and weaknesses; and more specific neuropsychological tests to complement the primary cognitive and achievement testing.

Moving into personality, social, emotional, and behavioral characteristics, it is good practice to obtain data from multiple sources, using instruments such as the Achenbach System of Empirically Based Assessment (Achenbach & Rescorla, 2003). For high-impact, specific types of dysfunction, such as moderate to severe attention deficits, autism spectrum symptoms, or schizotypal symptoms, specialized questionnaires designed for these narrow foci can be added to the battery. The MMPI–2–RF is then interpreted in the context of these other sources of data; indeed, because of the broad and comprehensive nature of the MMPI–2–RF hierarchical organization, it tends to serve as a global framework for the interpretation of data from other sources as well.

In some situations, it is possible to do a limited assessment using only a brief case review, a relatively abbreviated clinical interview, and just the MMPI–2–RF. This practice has been labeled a *consult–liaison service* and has been most common in training hospitals associated with medical schools. The person initiating the request for an assessment is another health care professional, such as a neurologist, surgeon, obstetrician, or other physician. The service structure is that the other professional is not actually referring the client or patient to the psychologist but is requesting a consultation regarding certain aspects of the case, for which the referring professional will continue to have primary responsibility. The MMPI–2–RF is uniquely suited to this context, particularly in terms of the very thorough, systematic interpretive framework presented in this book. In a total professional engagement of 2 hours or less, the psychologist can discuss the key questions with the professional making the request, review key aspects of the case, engage the patient in a brief interview (20–30 minutes) that will commonly follow an established rubric for the particular setting, and then administer and interpret the MMPI–2–RF. Psychologists are able to thus contribute highly accurate, unique information to the case that most likely would not be available to the principal professional otherwise.

As an example of another context in which this interpretive model works well, I and my colleagues have established a consult–liaison service with the counseling center at our university. The staff is a mix of psychologists, counselors, and social workers, all of whom focus on brief therapeutic intervention. They do not have the staffing or the time to conduct full psychological evaluations. So, in collaboration with the psychology clinic, any staff therapist may request an MMPI–2–RF consultation for a client. Our graduate student trainee discusses the questions and issues with the therapist, then meets and interviews the client. The MMPI–2–RF report is generally about a page and a half long, and the psychology student discusses the results in a joint session with the therapist and client. This program has been very successful, enthusiastically received and appreciated by the student counseling center. It is also a very gratifying role for the student psychologist. Readers may want to consider the possibilities of establishing focused consultations with other professionals in their general setting using the MMPI–2–RF as the data source.

In conclusion, the MMPI–2–RF is accurately seen as a leading-edge, state-of-the-art psychological assessment instrument. It rests on the most current models of psychopathology and, indeed, contributes to the ongoing development of theory in this field. Reconceptualizing psychopathology as a hierarchical organization of dimensional constructs ranging from relatively broad to relatively narrow in focus gives psychologists a way to fully capture the unique individual variation in each of our clients. This process is both more sensitive to the whole person and far more accurate than assigning individuals to any predetermined category. There will be revisions and future versions of the MMPI. However, the paradigm has shifted with the Restructured Form, and changes in the future will certainly be consistent with the broad framework provided in this book.

Glossary

This glossary provides brief definitions or descriptions of the abbreviations and technical terms found in this book. This list of terms relevant to users of the Minnesota Multiphasic Personality Inventory—2—Restructured Form (MMPI–2–RF) is not comprehensive, but it reflects an effort to identify the terms that are most important and that are perhaps most likely to be unclear to newcomers to the MMPI.

ACQUIESCENCE. Characteristic of a response set reflecting a tendency to agree with the item, regardless of content, by responding true. See *TRIN-r*.

ACT. Abbreviation for the Activation scale (Behavioral/Externalizing domain). Content describes heightened excitation and energy, mood swings, and lack of sleep.

AES. Abbreviation for the Aesthetic–Literary Interests scale. Content describes interests of an artistic nature, such as writing, music, or theater.

AGG. Abbreviation for the Aggression scale (Behavioral/Externalizing domain). Content describes engagement in physically aggressive, violent behavior.

AGGR-r. Abbreviation for the PSY-5 scale Aggressiveness–Revised (Behavioral/Externalizing domain). Content describes interpersonal dominance, assertiveness, and instrumental aggressiveness.

ANP. Abbreviation for the Anger Proneness scale (Emotional/Internalizing domain). Content describes anger and anger-related experiences.

AXY. Abbreviation for the Anxiety scale (Emotional/Internalizing domain). Content describes experiences of anxiety, fright, and nightmares.

BRF. Abbreviation for the Behavior-Restricting Fears scale (Emotional/Internalizing domain). Content describes fears that restrict normal activity, both in and outside of the home.

BXD. Abbreviation for the Behavioral/Externalizing Dysfunction scale, one of the three Higher-Order scales (Behavioral/Externalizing domain). Content describes maladaptive behaviors, including aggression, stealing, lying, interpersonal conflicts, and conflicts with authorities.

CNS. Abbreviation for the Cannot Say score or count, which is simply the raw count of items that could not be scored, most commonly by omission. This count is considered along with the nine Protocol Validity scales.

COG. Abbreviation for the Cognitive Complaints scale (Somatic/Cognitive domain). Content describes a diffuse pattern of cognitive difficulties (e.g., memory, concentration).

CONTENT VALIDITY. Degree to which the content of the items on the scale represents the content domain of the construct being measured.

CRITERION VALIDITY. Degree to which the score on the scale correlates with construct-relevant external criteria.

DISC-r. Abbreviation for the PSY-5 scale Disconstraint–Revised (Behavioral/Externalizing domain). Content describes impulsivity, excitement seeking, and undercontrolled behavior.

DSF. Abbreviation for the Disaffiliativeness scale (Interpersonal Functioning domain). Content reflects dislike of people and preference to be alone.

EID. Abbreviation for the Emotional/Internalizing Dysfunction scale, one of the three Higher-Order scales (Emotional/Internalizing domain). Content spans a broad range of emotional and internalizing problems, including sadness, depression, fear, stress, and anxiety.

FBS-r. Abbreviation for the Symptom Validity scale, one of the Protocol Validity scales, used to assess overreporting of somatic and cognitive problems.

FML. Abbreviation for the Family Problems scale (Interpersonal Functioning domain). Content reflects conflictual family relationships and lack of support from family.

Fp-r. Abbreviation for the Infrequent Psychopathology Responses scale, one of the Protocol Validity scales. Elevations reflect a tendency to overreport psychological symptoms specifically in comparison with a group with genuine severe psychopathology.

F-r. Abbreviation for the Infrequent Responses scale, one of the Protocol Validity scales. Elevations reflect a tendency to overreport a wide range of psychological, cognitive, and somatic symptoms.

Fs. Abbreviation for the Infrequent Somatic Responses scale, one of the Protocol Validity scales. Elevations reflect a tendency to overreport somatic symptoms in comparison with a group with genuine physical diseases.

GIC. Abbreviation for the Gastrointestinal Complaints scale (Somatic/Cognitive domain). Content describes a variety of gastrointestinal problems.

HLP. Abbreviation for the Helplessness/Hopelessness scale (Emotional/Internalizing domain). Content describes feelings of hopelessness, helplessness, and being overwhelmed.

HPC. Abbreviation for the Head Pain Complaints scale (Somatic/Cognitive domain). Content describes various head and neck pain complaints.

INTR-r. Abbreviation for the PSY-5 scale Introversion/Low Positive Emotionality–Revised (Emotional/Internalizing domain). Elevations suggest anhedonia, restricted interests, and social disengagement.

IPP. Abbreviation for the Interpersonal Passivity scale (Interpersonal Functioning domain). Content describes submissive, passive, and unassertive interpersonal interactions.

JCP. Abbreviation for the Juvenile Conduct Problems scale (Behavioral/Externalizing domain). Content describes past problematic behavior such as stealing, truancy, and negative peers.

K-r. Abbreviation for the Adjustment Validity scale, one of the Protocol Validity scales. Elevations suggest possible underreporting of psychopathology.

KRAEPELINIAN CATEGORIES. Model of psychopathology developed by German psychiatrist Emil Kraepelin (1856–1926) that is clearly reflected in the *Diagnostic and Statistical Manual of Mental Disorders* and the *International Classification of Diseases.*

L-r. Abbreviation for the Uncommon Virtues scale, one of the Protocol Validity scales. Elevations suggest possible underreporting of psychopathology.

MEASUREMENT ERROR. Difference between the theoretical true score or level of a trait in a given client and the observed score he or she obtained.

MEC. Abbreviation for the Mechanical–Physical Interests scale. Content describes interests in physical and mechanical activities, such as building things, farming, hunting, or sports.

MLS. Abbreviation for the Malaise scale (Somatic/Cognitive domain). Content describes a broad, general sense of poor health, weakness, and physical debilitation.

MSF. Abbreviation for the Multiple Specific Fears scale (Emotional/Internalizing domain). Content assess anxiety-producing fears of specific objects or situations.

NEGE-r. Abbreviation for the PSY-5 scale Negative Emotionality/Neuroticism–Revised (Emotional/Internalizing domain). Content describes a wide range of negative emotional experiences, including anxiety, insecurity, and worry.

NFC. Abbreviation for the Inefficacy scale (Emotional/Internalizing domain). Elevations indicate difficulty with making decisions and dealing effectively with challenges.

NONGENDERED NORMS. Norms for converting raw scores to *T* scores for the MMPI–2–RF based on a combined-gender sample. The original MMPI and MMPI–2 used gender-specific norms.

NUC. Abbreviation for the Neurological Complaints scale (Somatic/Cognitive domain). Content describes various neurological complaints (e.g., dizziness, numbness).

PSY-5. Personality Psychopathology Five scales.

PSYC-r. Abbreviation for the PSY-5 scale Psychoticism–Revised (Thought Dysfunction domain). Content describes symptoms associated with thought disturbance.

RAW SCORE. Count of the number of items endorsed in the scored direction by the client on a given scale.

RBS. Abbreviation for the Response Bias Scale, a Protocol Validity scale that is specifically sensitive to the overreporting of memory-related problems.

RC1. Abbreviation for the Somatic Complaints scale (Somatic/Cognitive domain). Content describes a wide range of physical symptoms and complaints.

RC2. Abbreviation for the Low Positive Emotions scale (Emotional/Internalizing domain). Elevations suggested the presence of anhedonia and lack of interest.

RC3. Abbreviation for the Cynicism scale (Interpersonal Functioning domain). High scores reflect a negative view of human nature.

RC4. Abbreviation for the Antisocial Behavior scale (Behavioral/Externalizing domain). Content describes various antisocial behaviors and related family conflict.

RC6. Abbreviation for the Ideas of Persecution scale (Thought Dysfunction domain). Content reflects self-referential delusions of persecution by others.

RC7. Abbreviation for the Dysfunctional Negative Emotions scale (Emotional/Internalizing domain). Elevations indicate a variety of negative emotional experiences, including anxiety, fear, stress, and anger.

RC8. Abbreviation for the Aberrant Experiences scale (Thought Dysfunction domain). Content includes unusual thinking and unusual perceptual experiences.

RC9. Abbreviation for the Hypomanic Activation scale (Behavioral/Externalizing domain). Content describes a wide range of emotional, behavioral, and thought characteristics associated with hypomanic activation.

RCd. Abbreviation for the Demoralization scale (Emotional/Internalizing domain). Elevations indicate general unhappiness, distress, and dissatisfaction with life.

RELIABILITY. Consistency of a measure; degree to which similar scores are achieved each time the measure is taken.

SAV. Abbreviation for the Social Avoidance scale (Interpersonal Functioning domain). Content reflects a preference to avoid social situations and lack of enjoyment of social events.

SFD. Abbreviation for the Self-Doubt scale (Emotional/Internalizing domain). Elevations indicate lack of confidence and feelings of uselessness, insecurity, and inferiority.

SHY. Abbreviation for the Shyness scale (Interpersonal Functioning domain). Content describes shyness, ability to be easily embarrassed, social anxiety, and discomfort around others.

STW. Abbreviation for the Stress/Worry scale (Emotional/Internalizing domain). Content describes experiences of stress and worry and problems with time pressure.

SUB. Abbreviation for the Substance Abuse scale (Behavioral/Externalizing domain). Content describes significant past and current substance abuse.

SUI. Abbreviation for the Suicidal/Death Ideation scale (Emotional/Internalizing domain). Content describes suicidal thoughts, intention, attempts, and history.

T SCORE. Standard score that reflects the deviation from the mean of the normative group. *T* scores have a mean of 50 and standard deviation of 10.

THD. Abbreviation for the Thought Dysfunction scale, one of the three Higher-Order scales (Thought Dysfunction domain). Elevations suggest difficulties with abnormal thinking processes.

TRIN-r. Abbreviation for the True Response Inconsistency scale, one of the Protocol Validity scales, a measure of inconsistency characterized by fixed responding (acquiescent or nonacquiescent).

UNIFORM *T* SCORE. Special form of the standard *T* score that preserves the positive skew of the raw score distributions and equates the level of skewness across scales. This transformation produces standard scores that are directly comparable with one another in terms of clinical significance.

VALIDITY. Extent to which a scale measures what it is intended to measure.

VRIN-r. Abbreviation for the Variable Response Inconsistency scale, one of the Protocol Validity scales; a measure of intentional or unintentional random responding.

References

Achenbach, T. M., & Rescorla, L. A. (2003). *Manual for the ASEBA adult forms and profiles.* Burlington: University of Vermont, Research Center for Children, Youth, and Families.

American Psychiatric Association. (2013). *Diagnostic and statistical manual of mental disorders* (5th ed.). Arlington, VA: Author.

Arbisi, P. A., Sellbom, M., & Ben-Porath, Y. S. (2008). Empirical correlates of the MMPI–2 Restructured Clinical (RC) Scales in psychiatric inpatients. *Journal of Personality Assessment, 90,* 122–128. http://dx.doi.org/10.1080/00223890701845146

Arce, R., Fariña, F., Seijo, D., & Novo, M. (2015). Assessing impression management with the MMPI–2 in child custody litigation. *Assessment, 22,* 769–777. http://dx.doi.org/10.1177/1073191114558111

Archer, R. P., Handel, R. W., Ben-Porath, Y. S., & Tellegen, A. (2016). *MMPI–A–RF (Minnesota Multiphasic Personality Inventory—Adolescent Restructured Form) administration, scoring, interpretation, and technical manual.* Minneapolis: University of Minnesota Press.

Bagby, R. M., Nicholson, R. A., Bacchiochi, J. R., Ryder, A. G., & Bury, A. S. (2002). The predictive capacity of the MMPI–2 and PAI validity scales and indexes to detect coached and uncoached feigning. *Journal of Personality Assessment, 78,* 69–86. http://dx.doi.org/10.1207/S15327752JPA7801_05

Bandura, A. (1977). Self-efficacy: Toward a unifying theory of behavioral change. *Psychological Review, 84,* 191–215.

Ben-Porath, Y. S. (2012a). Addressing challenges to MMPI–2–RF-based testimony: Questions and answers. *Archives of Clinical Neuropsychology, 27,* 691–705. http://dx.doi.org/10.1093/arclin/acs083

Ben-Porath, Y. S. (2012b). *Interpreting the MMPI–2–RF*. Minneapolis: University of Minnesota Press.

Ben-Porath, Y. S., & Tellegen, A. (2008/2011). *MMPI–2–RF (Minnesota Multiphasic Personality Inventory—2—Restructured Form) manual for administration, scoring, and interpretation*. Minneapolis: University of Minnesota Press.

Block, A. R., Ben-Porath, Y. S., & Marek, R. J. (2013). Psychological risk factors for poor outcome of spine surgery and spinal cord stimulator implant: A review of the literature and their assessment with the MMPI–2–RF. *The Clinical Neuropsychologist, 27*, 81–107. http://dx.doi.org/10.1080/13854046.2012.721007

Butcher, J. N., Dahlstrom, W. G., Graham, J. R., Tellegen, A., & Kaemmer, B. (1989). *Manual for the restandardized Minnesota Multiphasic Personality Inventory: MMPI–2*. Minneapolis: University of Minnesota Press.

Butcher, J. N., Graham, J. R., Williams, C. L., & Ben-Porath, Y. S. (1990). *Development and use of the MMPI–2 Content Scales*. Minneapolis: University of Minnesota Press.

Dahlstrom, W. G., & Welsh, G. S. (1960). *An MMPI handbook: A guide to use in clinical practice and research*. Minneapolis: University of Minnesota Press.

Dahlstrom, W. G., Welsh, G. S., & Dahlstrom, L. E. (1972). *An MMPI handbook, Volume 1: Clinical interpretation*. Minneapolis: University of Minnesota Press.

Dahlstrom, W. G., Welsh, G. S., & Dahlstrom, L. E. (1975). *An MMPI handbook, Volume 2: Research developments and applications*. Minneapolis: University of Minnesota Press.

Dragon, W. R., Ben-Porath, Y. S., & Handel, R. W. (2012). Examining the impact of unscorable item responses on the validity and interpretability of MMPI–2/MMPI–2–RF Restructured Clinical (RC) Scale scores. *Assessment, 19*, 101–113. http://dx.doi.org/10.1177/1073191111415362

Franz, A. O., Harrop, T. M., & McCord, D. M. (2017). Examining the construct validity of the MMPI–2–RF Interpersonal Functioning scales using the Computerized Adaptive Test of Personality Disorder as a comparative framework. *Journal of Personality Assessment, 99*, 416–423. http://dx.doi.org/10.1080/00223891.2016.1222394

Friedman, A. F., Bolinskey, P. K., Levak, R. W., & Nichols, D. S. (2015). *Psychological assessment with the MMPI–2/MMPI–2–RF*. New York, NY: Routledge.

Gervais, R. O., Ben-Porath, Y. S., & Wygant, D. B. (2009). Empirical correlates and interpretation of the MMPI–2–RF Cognitive Complaints Scale. *The Clinical Neuropsychologist, 23*, 996–1015. http://dx.doi.org/10.1080/13854040902748249

Glassmire, D. M., Tarescavage, A. M., Burchett, D., Martinez, J., & Gomez, A. (2016). Clinical utility of the MMPI–2–RF SUI items and scale in a forensic inpatient setting: Association with interview self-report and future suicidal behavior. *Psychological Assessment, 28*, 1502–1509. http://dx.doi.org/10.1037/pas0000220

Gottfried, E., Bodell, L., Carbonell, J., & Joiner, T. (2014). The clinical utility of the MMPI–2–RF Suicidal/Death Ideation Scale. *Psychological Assessment, 26*, 1205–1211. http://dx.doi.org/10.1037/pas0000017

Graham, J. R. (1977). *The MMPI: A practical guide*. New York, NY: Oxford University Press.

Graham, J. R. (2011). *MMPI–2: Assessing personality and psychopathology* (5th ed.). New York, NY: Oxford University Press.

Greene, R. L. (2011). *The MMPI–2/MMPI–2–RF: An interpretive manual* (3rd ed.). Boston, MA: Pearson.

Grossi, L. M., Green, D., Belfi, B., McGrath, R. E., Griswold, H., & Schreiber, J. (2015). Identifying aggression in forensic inpatients using the MMPI–2–RF: An examination of MMPI–2–RF scale scores and estimated psychopathy indices. *The International Journal of Forensic Mental Health, 14,* 231–244. http://dx.doi.org/10.1080/14999013.2015.1108943

Handel, R. W., Ben-Porath, Y. S., Tellegen, A., & Archer, R. P. (2010). Psychometric functioning of the MMPI–2–RF VRIN-r and TRIN-r scales with varying degrees of randomness, acquiescence, and counter-acquiescence. *Psychological Assessment, 22,* 87–95. http://dx.doi.org/10.1037/a0017061

Harkness, A. R., Finn, J. A., McNulty, J. L., & Shields, S. M. (2012). The Personality Psychopathology—Five (PSY–5): Recent constructive replication and assessment literature review. *Psychological Assessment, 24,* 432–443. http://dx.doi.org/10.1037/a0025830

Harkness, A. R., & McNulty, J. L. (1994). The Personality Psychopathology Five (PSY–5): Issue from the pages of a diagnostic manual instead of a dictionary. In S. Strack & M. Lorr (Eds.), *Differentiating normal and abnormal personality* (pp. 291–315). New York, NY: Springer.

Harkness, A. R., McNulty, J. L., & Ben-Porath, Y. S. (1995). The Personality Psychopathology Five (PSY–5): Constructs and MMPI–2 scales. *Psychological Assessment, 7,* 104–114. http://dx.doi.org/10.1037/1040-3590.7.1.104

Harkness, A. R., McNulty, J. L., Finn, J. A., Reynolds, S. M., Shields, S. M., & Arbisi, P. (2014). The MMPI–2–RF Personality Psychopathology Five (PSY–5–RF) scales: Development and validity research. *Journal of Personality Assessment, 96,* 140–150. http://dx.doi.org/10.1080/00223891.2013.823439

Hathaway, S. R., & McKinley, J. C. (1940). A multiphasic personality schedule (Minnesota): I. Construction of the schedule. *Journal of Psychology, 10,* 249–254. http://dx.doi.org/10.1080/00223980.1940.9917000

Henry, G. K., Heilbronner, R. L., Mittenberg, W., Enders, C., & Domboski, K. (2009). Comparison of the MMPI–2 restructured Demoralization Scale, Depression Scale, and Malingered Mood Disorder Scale in identifying non-credible symptom reporting in personal injury litigants and disability claimants. *The Clinical Neuropsychologist, 23,* 153–166. http://dx.doi.org/10.1080/13854040801969524

Ingram, P. B., & Ternes, M. S. (2016). The detection of content-based invalid responding: A meta-analysis of the MMPI–2–Restructured Form's (MMPI–2–RF) over-reporting validity scales. *The Clinical Neuropsychologist, 30,* 473–496. http://dx.doi.org/10.1080/13854046.2016.1187769

Insel, T. R. (2013, April 29). *Post by former NIMH Director Thomas Insel: Transforming diagnosis.* Bethesda, MD: National Institute of Mental Health. Retrieved from https://www.nimh.nih.gov/about/directors/thomas-insel/blog/2013/transforming-diagnosis.shtml

Insel, T. R. (2014). The NIMH Research Domain Criteria (RDoC) project: Precision medicine for psychiatry. *The American Journal of Psychiatry, 171,* 395–397. http://dx.doi.org/10.1176/appi.ajp.2014.14020138

Judge, T. A., Erez, A., Bono, J. E., & Thoresen, C. J. (2002). Are measures of self-esteem, neuroticism, locus of control, and generalized self-efficacy indicators of a common core construct? *Journal of Personality and Social Psychology, 83*, 693–710.

Kotov, R., Ruggero, C. J., Krueger, R. F., Watson, D., Yuan, Q., & Zimmerman, M. (2011). New dimensions in the quantitative classification of mental illness. *Archives of General Psychiatry, 68*, 1003–1011. http://dx.doi.org/10.1001/archgenpsychiatry.2011.107

Krueger, R. F. (1999). The structure of common mental disorders. *Archives of General Psychiatry, 56*, 921–926. http://dx.doi.org/10.1001/archpsyc.56.10.921

Marek, R. J., Block, A. R., & Ben-Porath, Y. S. (2015). The Minnesota Multiphasic Personality Inventory—2—Restructured Form (MMPI–2–RF): Incremental validity in predicting early post-operative outcomes in spine surgery candidates. *Psychological Assessment, 27*, 114–124. http://dx.doi.org/10.1037/pas0000035

McCord, D. M., & Drerup, L. C. (2011). Relative practical utility of the MMPI–2 RC Scales versus the Clinical Scales in a chronic pain patient sample. *Journal of Clinical and Experimental Neuropsychology, 33*, 140–146. http://dx.doi.org/10.1080/13803395.2010.495056

McCrae, R. R., & Costa, P. T., Jr. (2008). The five-factor theory of personality. In O. P. John, R. W. Robins, & L. A. Pervin (Eds.), *Handbook of personality: Theory and research* (3rd ed., pp. 159–181). New York, NY: Guilford Press.

Myers, L., Fleming, M., Lancman, M., Perrine, K., & Lancman, M. (2013). Stress coping strategies in patients with psychogenic non-epileptic seizures and how they relate to trauma symptoms, alexithymia, anger and mood. *Seizure, 22*, 634–639. http://dx.doi.org/10.1016/j.seizure.2013.04.018

Pearson. (2014). *Case description: Mr. D—Bariatric surgery candidate score report.* San Antonio, TX: Author. Retrieved from http://images.pearsonclinical.com/images/Assets/MMPI-2-RF/MMPI-2-RF_Score_Bariatric.pdf

Regents of the University of Minnesota. (2012). *MMPI–2–RF interpretation worksheet.* Minneapolis: Author. Retrieved from http://www.upress.umn.edu/test-division/mtdda/webdocs/forms/mmpi-2-rf-worksheet

Sellbom, M. (2012). The MMPI–2–RF is ready for the Daubert challenge: Evidence, implications, and recommendations for use in court testimony. *Journal of Psychological Practice, 17*, 151–179.

Sellbom, M., & Bagby, R. M. (2008). Validity of the MMPI–2–RF (restructured form) L-r and K-r Scales in detecting underreporting in clinical and nonclinical samples. *Psychological Assessment, 20*, 370–376. http://dx.doi.org/10.1037/a0012952

Sellbom, M., & Bagby, R. M. (2010). Detection of overreported psychopathology with the MMPI–2–RF [corrected] validity scales. *Psychological Assessment, 22*, 757–767. http://dx.doi.org/10.1037/a0020825

Sellbom, M., Ben-Porath, Y. S., & Bagby, R. M. (2008). On the hierarchical structure of mood and anxiety disorders: Confirmatory evidence and elaboration of a model of temperament markers. *Journal of Abnormal Psychology, 117*, 576–590. http://dx.doi.org/10.1037/a0012536

Sellbom, M., Toomey, A., Wygant, D., Kucharski, L. T., & Duncan, S. (2010). Utility of the MMPI–2–RF (Restructured Form) validity scales in detecting malingering in a criminal forensic setting: A known-groups design. *Psychological Assessment, 22,* 22–31. http://dx.doi.org/10.1037/a0018222

Simms, L. J., Goldberg, L. R., Roberts, J. E., Watson, D., Welte, J., & Rotterman, J. H. (2011). Computerized adaptive assessment of personality disorder: Introducing the CAT–PD project. *Journal of Personality Assessment, 93,* 380–389. http://dx.doi.org/10.1080/00223891.2011.577475

Sleep, C. C., Petty, J. A., & Wygant, D. B. (2015). Framing the results: Assessment of response bias through select self-report measures in psychological injury evaluations. *Psychological Injury and Law, 8,* 27–39. http://dx.doi.org/10.1007/s12207-015-9219-1

Solomon, D., Morgan, B., Asberg, K., & McCord, D. (2014). Treatment implications based on measures of child abuse potential and parental mental health: Are we missing an intervention opportunity? *Children and Youth Services Review, 43,* 153–159. http://dx.doi.org/10.1016/j.childyouth.2014.05.016

Tarescavage, A. M., Brewster, J., Corey, D. M., & Ben-Porath, Y. S. (2015). Use of pre-hire Minnesota Multiphasic Personality Inventory—2—Restructured Form (MMPI–2–RF) police candidate scores to predict supervisor ratings of posthire performance. *Assessment, 22,* 411–428. http://dx.doi.org/10.1177/1073191114548445

Tellegen, A. (1985). Structures of mood and personality and their relevance to assessing anxiety, with an emphasis on self-report. In A. H. Tuma & J. D. Maser (Eds.), *Anxiety and the anxiety disorders* (pp. 681–706). Hillsdale, NJ: Erlbaum.

Tellegen, A., & Ben-Porath, Y. S. (2008/2011). *MMPI–2–RF (Minnesota Multiphasic Personality Inventory—2 Restructured Form) technical manual.* Minneapolis: University of Minnesota Press.

Tellegen, A., Ben-Porath, Y. S., McNulty, J. L., Arbisi, P. A., Graham, J. R., & Kaemmer, B. (2003). *MMPI–2 Restructured Clinical (RC) Scales: Development, validation, and interpretation.* Minneapolis: University of Minnesota Press.

University of Minnesota Press. (2017). *MMPI-2-RF references by topic.* Minneapolis: Author. Retrieved from https://www.upress.umn.edu/test-division/mtdda/webdocs/references.pdf

Watson, D., Kotov, R., & Gamez, W. (2006). Basic dimensions of temperament in relation to personality and psychopathology. In R. F. Krueger & J. L. Tacket (Eds.), *Personality and psychopathology* (pp. 7–38). New York, NY: Guilford Press.

Welsh, G. S., & Dahlstrom, W. G. (Eds.). (1956). *Basic readings on the MMPI in psychology and medicine.* Minneapolis: University of Minnesota Press.

World Health Organization. (1992). *The ICD–10 classification of mental and behavioural disorders: Clinical descriptions and diagnostic guidelines.* Geneva, Switzerland: Author.

Wygant, D. B., Ben-Porath, Y. S., & Arbisi, P. A. (2004, May). *Development and initial validation of a scale to detect somatic over-reporting.* Poster presented at the 39th Annual Symposium on Recent Developments of the MMPI–2/MMPI–A, Minneapolis, MN.

Index

A

Aberrant Experiences scale (*RC8*)
  breadth of, 61
  in case example, 106
  content and interpretation of, 63–64
  as Critical Scale, 16
  and Hypomanic Activation scale, 69
  in interpretation procedure, 80, 85
  on Score Report, 26
  and Thought Dysfunction scale, 61, 62
Abuse, child, 112
Achenbach System of Empirically Based Assessment, 112
Acquiescence, 32, 41, 42
Acting-out behaviors, 65, 67
Activation scale (*ACT*)
  breadth of, 65
  content and interpretation of, 69–70
  and Juvenile Conduct Problems scale, 67
Adjustment, positive, 43
Adjustment Validity measure (*K-r*)
  in case example, 90
  content and interpretation of, 39–40, 40*t*
  fixed responding and, 42
  in interpretation procedure, 80
  random responding and, 42
  and Substantive Scales, 38
  underreporting and scores on, 43
Administration, 19–23
  client issues influencing, 20–21
  computer-assisted, 21–22, 28
  group, 23
  iPad, 21
  standard instructions and procedures, 22–23
  standard modalities, 21–22
Administrators, 19–22
Adolescents, MMPI for, 4, 20
Aesthetic–Literary Interests scale (*AES*), 76
Age, client, 20
Aggression scale (*AGG*)
  and Anger Proneness score, 58
  breadth of, 65
  content and interpretation of, 69
  as Critical Scale, 16
  in interpretation procedure, 81
  and Juvenile Conduct Problems scale, 67
  on Score Report, 26
Aggressiveness–Revised scale (*AGGR-r*)
  and Anger Proneness score, 58
  in case example, 106
  content and interpretation of, 70
  and Juvenile Conduct Problems scale, 67
  as PSY-5 Scale, 65
AGGR-r. See Aggressiveness–Revised scale
Agoraphobic dysfunction, 59
Alcohol abuse, 67
American Psychiatric Association (ApA), 107. *See also Diagnostic and Statistical Manual of Mental Disorders (DSM)*
American Psychological Association (APA), 4–5

Anger, 69
Anger management treatment, 59
Anger Proneness scale (*ANP*), 51, 58–59
Anger-related disorders, 59
Anhedonia
 and Hypomanic Activation score, 68
 Interest Scales scores and, 76, 86
 in three-factor model for internalizing dysfunction, 50, 55, 84
Anhedonia (CAT-PD), 74, 75
ANP (Anger Proneness scale), 51, 58–59
Antianxiety medication, 58, 61
Antidepressant medications, 55, 56
Antipsychotic medication, 62–64
Antisocial Behavior scale (*RC4*)
 breadth of, 65, 71–72
 in case example, 103, 106
 content and interpretation of, 66–67
 in interpretation procedure, 85
 and Juvenile Conduct Problems scale, 67
 marijuana use and scores on, 104
Antisocial personality disorder, 65–67
Anxiety, social, 74
Anxiety disorders, 59
Anxiety/Fear (factor), 50, 56, 84
Anxiety scale (*AXY*)
 breadth of, 51
 in case example, 103, 104, 106
 content and interpretation of, 58
 as Critical Scale, 16
 in interpretation procedure, 80
 on Score Report, 26
Anxiousness (CAT-PD), 75
ApA (American Psychiatric Association), 107
APA (American Psychological Association), 4–5
Arbisi, P. A., 11, 35
Archer, R. P., 29
Audio version of MMPI–2–RF, 21
Avoidant personality disorder, 54, 75
AXY. See Anxiety scale

B
Back F measure (*Fb*), 29
Bad, faking, 33
Bagby, R. M., 29
Bandura, A., 54
Bariatric surgery, 111
Behavior(s). *See also* Antisocial Behavior scale (*RC4*)
 acting-out, 65, 67
 interpersonally aggressive, 70
 maladaptive. *See* Externalizing domain
 physically aggressive, 69
Behavioral/Externalizing Dysfunction scale (*BXD*), 14
 breadth of, 65
 in case example, 103, 106
 content and interpretation of, 65–66
 and Disconstraint–Revised scale, 71
 in interpretation procedure, 85
 and Juvenile Conduct Problems scale, 67
 marijuana use and scores on, 104
Behavior-Restricting Fears scale (*BRF*), 51, 59
Ben-Porath, Y. S., 4–6, 11, 13, 16, 19, 29, 35, 50, 81, 88, 107, 112
Bolinskey, P. K., 10
Booklet, MMPI–2–RF, 21
Borderline personality disorder, 54
BRF (Behavior-Restricting Fears scale), 51, 59
Broad scales, 3, 4, 45
Butcher, James, 11
BXD. See Behavioral/Externalizing Dysfunction scale

C
Callousness (CAT-PD), 75
Cannot Say measure (*CNS*)
 in case example, 90, 104, 105
 content and interpretation of, 30–31, 31*t*
 in interpretation procedure, 79, 81, 82
 on MMPI, 29
 and nonresponding, 30, 41
 and overreporting, 42
 on Score Report, 25
 scoring of, 28
Categorical model of psychopathology, 9, 12, 13, 87
CAT-PD (Computerized Adaptive Test of Personality Disorder), 73–75
Child abuse, 112
Child custody, 112
Chronic pain, 111
Client factors, in administration, 20–21
Clinical Scales
 and categorical vs. dimensional model of psychopathology, 13
 item-level information on, 26
 on MMPI, 9, 11
 restructuring of, 11–12. *See also* Restructured Clinical (RC) Scales
CNS. See Cannot Say measure
Cognitive Complaints scale (*COG*), 46, 49, 83
Cognitive domain. *See* Somatic/Cognitive domain
Cognitive problems, 42
College student counseling centers, 27, 113
College students, comparison group of, 27
Comparison groups, 10–11, 27, 82, 104
Comprehensive assessment, 112
Computer-assisted administration, 21–22, 28
Computer-assisted scoring, 23–24, 28
Computer-generated reports, 25–27
Computerized Adaptive Test of Personality Disorder (CAT-PD), 73–75
Computerized Assessment of Response Bias, 36
Conduct disorders, 65
Conscientiousness, 65, 71

Consult–liaison service, 112–113
Content-based response biases, 41
Content Component Scales (MMPI), 10
Content nonresponsiveness
  defined, 30, 41
  interpretation procedure to evaluate, 82
  scales indicating, 30–32
Content Scales (MMPI), 10, 13
Content validity, 5
Conversion disorder, 47
Correction measure (*K*), 29
Criterion validity, 5
Critical Scales
  availability of, 21
  in interpretation procedure, 80, 81
  item-level information on, 25–26
  and psychometric considerations, 16
Cross-scale correlations, 17
Custody cases, 112
Cutoff scores
  in case example, 104
  and comparison groups, 27
  for Critical Scales, 26
  for Protocol Validity scales, 25, 41, 90
Cynicism, 62
Cynicism scale (*RC3*)
  and Anger Proneness score, 58
  breadth of, 72
  content and interpretation of, 73
  and Neurological Complaints score, 49
  and Somatic Complaints score, 47

D

Dahlstrom, W. G., 10, 11
Delusions, 61, 62
Demoralization
  defined, 51–52
  and Paranoia Scale, 62
  in Restructured Clinical Scales, 11, 12
Demoralization/Distress (factor), 50, 84
Demoralization scale (*RCd*)
  breadth of, 50
  in case example, 103, 104, 106
  content and interpretation of, 51–52
  facet-level scales under, 51
  in interpretation procedure, 84
  and Low Positive Emotions score, 55
Dependent personality disorder, 74
Depression, 54, 55
Depression category (MMPI), 9
Depression-related disorders, 52, 55. *See also* Major depressive disorder
Depressivity/Anhedonia (factor), 50, 55, 84
Despair, 53
Diagnosis
  categorical vs. dimensional models of, 9, 12–14
  and narrative report, 87
Diagnostic and Statistical Manual of Mental Disorders (*DSM*), 12, 13, 59, 87, 107
Diagnostic Considerations section (Interpretation Worksheet), 107
Dichotomous choice, 23
Dimensional framework. *See also* Hierarchical–dimensional model
  in MMPI–2–RF, 3–4, 13–14
  Thought Dysfunction domain in, 61
Dimensional model of psychopathology, 13–14
Disaffiliativeness scale (*DSF*), 72, 75–76
Disconstraint, 65, 71
Disconstraint–Revised scale (*DISC-r*)
  in case example, 106
  content and interpretation of, 71
  and Juvenile Conduct Problems scale, 67
  marijuana use and scores on, 104
  as PSY-5 Scale, 65
DISC-r. See Disconstraint–Revised scale
Disengagement, social, 56
Disordered thinking, 63
Distress
  emotional, 51, 52, 61
  psychological, 52
  in three-factor model for internalizing dysfunction, 50, 84
Domineering (CAT-PD), 73
Drug abuse, 67
DSF (Disaffiliativeness scale), 72, 75–76
DSM. See Diagnostic and Statistical Manual of Mental Disorders
Duncan, S., 29
Dysfunctional Negative Emotions scale (*RC7*)
  breadth of, 50
  in case example, 103, 104, 106
  content and interpretation of, 56–57
  facet-level scales under, 51
  in interpretation procedure, 84
  and Negative Emotionality/Neuroticism–Revised scale, 60

E

EID. See Emotional/Internalizing Dysfunction scale
Emotional Detachment (CAT-PD), 75
Emotional distress, 51, 52, 61
Emotional/Internalizing Dysfunction scale (*EID*), 14
  breadth of, 50
  in case example, 103–106
  and Cognitive Complaints scale, 46
  content and interpretation of, 51
  in interpretation procedure, 84
Empirical keying, 9
Endnotes, Interpretive Report, 26
Energy level, 68–69
Exhibitionism (CAT-PD), 73, 74
Externalizing disorders, 66, 67

Externalizing domain, 3
Activation scale, 69–70
Aggression scale, 69
Aggressiveness–Revised scale, 70
Antisocial Behavior scale, 66–67
in assessment model, 8*f*, 9
Behavioral/Externalizing Dysfunction scale, 65–66
in case example, 90, 95*f*, 103, 106
description of, 64–65
Disconstraint–Revised scale, 71
Hypomanic Activation scale, 68–69
in interpretation procedure, 80–81, 85
Juvenile Conduct Problems scale, 67
and psychometric considerations with MMPI–2–RF, 16
scales within, 65–71
on Score Report, 25
Substance Abuse scale, 67–68
Externalizing dysfunction. *See* Behavioral/ Externalizing Dysfunction scale (*BXD*)

F
F (Infrequency measure), 29
Faking bad, 33
Faking good, 37
False (response)
answering both *true* and, 31
as fixed response, 30, 32, 42
and underreporting, 43
Family Problems scale (*FML*), 71, 72, 85
Fb (Back F) measure, 29
FBS-r. See Symptom Validity measure
Fear
Behavior-Restricting Fears scale, 51, 59
Multiple Specific Fears scale, 51, 59–60
in three-factor model for internalizing dysfunction, 50, 56, 84
Feigning (term), 33
Femininity, MMPI scale for, 9, 76
First pass review
in case example, 90, 103–104
conducting, 79–81
in two-pass approach, 77
Five-factor model of personality, 60, 64, 65, 71
Fixed responding, 30, 41, 42
FML. See Family Problems scale
Forensic settings, 27, 112
Formal interpretive statements, 45–46
Fp-r. See Infrequent Psychopathology Responses measure
F-r. See Infrequent Responses measure
Franz, A. O., 71
Friedman, A. F., 10
Fs. See Infrequent Somatic Responses measure
Full psychological report, 85–86, 108

G
Gamez, W., 13
Gastrointestinal Complaints scale (*GIC*)
breadth of, 46, 47
in case example, 103–105
content and interpretation of, 48
Gervais, R. O., 50
GIC. See Gastrointestinal Complaints scale
Good, faking, 37
Graham, Jack, 10, 11
Greene, Roger, 10
Group administration, 23

H
Hallucinations, 61
Handel, R. W., 29
Hand scoring, 23–24, 28
Harkness, A. R., 13, 61, 81
Harrop, T. M., 71
Hathaway, Starke, 9, 10
Head Pain Complaints scale (*HPC*), 46–49
Helplessness/Hopelessness scale (*HLP*)
breadth of, 51
in case example, 103, 104
content and interpretation of, 53
as Critical Scale, 16
in interpretation procedure, 80
on Score Report, 26
Hierarchical–dimensional model. *See also* Interpretation of MMPI–2–RF
and item overlap, 17
in MMPI–2–RF, 4, 78*t*, 87
paradigm shift to, 13
and Score Report, 25
Higher-Order Scales, 12, 14
in case example, 90, 93*f*, 103
in Externalizing domain, 64–65, 71
in Internalizing domain, 50, 51
in interpretation procedure, 85
interpreting scores on, 80
item overlap and, 17
and RC scales, 62
on Score Report, 25
and Somatic/Cognitive domain, 46
in Thought Dysfunction domain, 61
Hippocrates, 12
History of prior testing, 20
HLP. See Helplessness/Hopelessness scale
Homosexuality, 76
Hostile Aggression (CAT-PD), 73
Hostility, 58
HPC (Head Pain Complaints scale), 46–49
Hypochondriasis, 9, 33
Hypomania category (MMPI), 9
Hypomanic Activation scale (*RC9*)
breadth of, 65
in case example, 103, 106

content and interpretation of, 68–69
in interpretation procedure, 85
and Juvenile Conduct Problems scale, 67
Hypomanic episodes, 69, 70
Hysteria category (MMPI), 9

I
ICD. *See International Classification of Diseases*
Ideas of Persecution scale (*RC6*)
breadth of, 61
in case example, 106
content and interpretation of, 62–63
as Critical Scale, 16
and Cynicism scale, 73
and Hypomanic Activation scale, 69
in interpretation procedure, 80, 85
on Score Report, 26
and Thought Dysfunction scale, 61, 62
Impulse control, 71
Inconsistent fixed responding, 41, 42
Inconsistent random responding, 41–42
Inconsistent responding, 38, 41–42
Independent validity, 84
Inefficacy scale (*NFC*)
breadth of, 51
in case example, 103
content and interpretation of, 54–55
and Self-Doubt scale, 54
Infrequency measure (*F*), 29
Infrequent Psychopathology Responses measure (*Fp-r*)
in case example, 90
content and interpretation of, 34–35, 35*t*
cutoff score for, 41
in interpretation procedure, 79
overreporting and score on, 43
random responding and, 42
Infrequent Responses measure (*F-r*)
in case example, 90
content and interpretation of, 33–34, 34*t*
cutoff score for, 41
overreporting and score on, 43
random responding and, 42
Infrequent Somatic Responses measure (*Fs*)
in case example, 90
content and interpretation of, 35, 36*t*
in interpretation procedure, 79
overreporting and scores on, 43
random responding and, 42
and Somatic/Cognitive domain scores, 46–47
and Symptom Validity scale, 36
Ingram, P. B., 29
Inpatient settings, 27, 111
Inpatient treatment, 26, 62–64
Instructions, standardized, 22–23
Intentional overreporting, 33
Intentional underreporting, 43
Interest Scales, 12
in case example, 90, 95*f*, 103, 107
description of, 76
interpreting scores on, 80–81, 86
T-scores for, 24
Internalizing disorders, 33, 51
Internalizing domain, 3
Anger Proneness scale, 58–59
Anxiety scale, 58
in assessment model, 8*f*, 9
Behavior-Restricting Fears scale, 59
in case example, 90, 94*f*, 103, 105–106
and Cognitive Complaints scale, 46
Demoralization scale, 51–52
description of, 50–51
Dysfunctional Negative Emotions scale, 56–57
Emotional/Internalizing Dysfunction scale, 51
Helplessness/Hopelessness scale, 53
Inefficacy scale, 54–55
in interpretation procedure, 80, 83–84
Introversion/Low Positive Emotionality–Revised scale, 56
Low Positive Emotions scale, 55
Multiple Specific Fears scale, 59–60
Negative Emotionality/Neuroticism–Revised scale, 60–61
and psychometric considerations with MMPI–2–RF, 16
scales within, 51–61
on Score Report, 25
Self-Doubt scale, 54
Stress/Worry scale, 57
Suicidal/Death Ideation scale, 52–53
Internalizing dysfunction
scale for measuring. *See* Emotional/Internalizing Dysfunction scale (*EID*)
three-factor model for, 50, 84
International Classification of Diseases (ICD), 12, 13, 87, 107
Interpersonal functioning, 85–86, 108
Interpersonal Functioning domain, 3, 4
in assessment model, 8*f*, 9
in case example, 90, 95*f*, 103, 107
in interpretation procedure, 80–81, 85–86
and psychometric considerations with MMPI–2–RF, 16
scales in, 71–76
on Score Report, 25
Interpersonally aggressive behavior, 70
Interpersonal Passivity scale (*IPP*)
breadth of, 72
in case example, 103, 107
content and interpretation of, 73–74
Interpersonal relationships, Substantive Scales and, 71

Interpretation case example, 89–109
background information, 89–90
Diagnostic Considerations, 107
first pass review, 90, 103–104
Higher-Order Scales, 103
Interest Scales, 103, 107
Interpretation Worksheet, 90, 99*f*–102*f*
item-level information, 104
narrative report, 108, 109*e*
Personality Psychopathology Five Scales, 103–104
Protocol Validity Scales, 90, 105
Restructured Clinical Scales, 103
Score Report, 90, 91*f*–98*f*
second pass review, 104–108
Substantive Scales, 103, 105–107
Treatment Considerations, 107–108
Interpretation of MMPI–2–RF, 5, 77–88. *See also* Interpretation case example
first pass review for, 79–81
Higher-Order Scales, 80
Interest Scales, 80–81, 86
overview, 78*t*
Personality Psychopathology Five Scales, 81
and preparing narrative report, 86–88
Protocol Validity Scales, 79–80, 82
Protocol Validity Scales in, 40–41
Restructured Clinical Scales, 80
second pass review for, 82–86
Substantive Scales, 80–81, 83–86
two-pass approach to, 3, 45, 77
Interpretation Worksheet, MMPI–2–RF. *See also specific sections*
for case example, 90, 99*f*–102*f*, 104–108, 109*e*
described, 79
Diagnostic Considerations section, 107
preparing, 82–86
preparing narrative report from, 86–88, 108, 109*e*
Substantive Scales on, 45
Treatment Considerations section, 107–108
in two-pass approach, 77
Interpreting the MMPI–2–RF (Ben-Porath), 4, 5
Interpretive Report, 25, 26, 28
Interpretive statements
on Interpretation Worksheet, 82, 83
official, 5
on Substantive Scales, 45–46
Introversion/Low Positive Emotionality–Revised scale (*INTR-r*)
breadth of, 51
in case example, 104, 106, 107
content and interpretation of, 56
and Interest Scales scores, 86
INTR-r. See Introversion/Low Positive Emotionality–Revised scale
iPad administration, 21
IPP. See Interpersonal Passivity scale
Item-level information
in case example, 98*f*, 104, 105
reporting of, 25–26

J

Juvenile Conduct Problems scale (*JCP*), 65–67
Juvenile delinquency, 67

K

K (Correction measure), 29
Kaemmer, Beverly, 11
Kent State University, 5
Kotov, R., 13
K-r. See Adjustment Validity measure
Kraepelin, Emil, 12
Kraepelinian diagnostic categories, 9, 12
Krueger, R. F., 13
Kucharski, L. T., 29

L

Levak, R. W., 10
Lie measure (*L*), 29
Low positive emotionality. *See* Introversion/Low Positive Emotionality–Revised scale (*INTR-r*)
Low Positive Emotions scale (*RC2*)
breadth of, 50
in case example, 103, 104, 106, 107
content and interpretation of, 55
facet-level scales under, 51
and Interest Scales scores, 86
in interpretation procedure, 84
Low self-esteem, 54
L-r. See Uncommon Virtues measure

M

Major depressive disorder, 55, 68, 76
Maladaptive behaviors. *See* Externalizing domain
Malaise scale (*MLS*), 46, 47, 105
Malingering, 29, 33, 37
Manic episodes, 69, 70
Marijuana use, 104
Masculinity/Femininity Scale (MMPI), 9, 76
McCord, D. M., 71
McKinley, J. C., 9
McNulty, J. L., 11, 13, 61, 81
Mechanical–Physical Interests scale (*MEC*), 76
Medical settings, 27, 111
Medications
antianxiety, 58, 61
antidepressant, 55, 56
antipsychotic, 62–64
mood-stabilizing, 69, 70
Memory problems, 36, 37
Midlevel scales, 3, 4

Minnesota Multiphasic Personality Inventory (MMPI)
administration of, 20
and categorical model of psychopathology, 12, 13
demoralization measures on, 52
evolution of, 14
history of, 9–10
Masculinity/Femininity Scale on, 76
MMPI–2–RF vs., 3
popularity of, 4, 7
protocol validity measures on, 29
settings for, 111
Minnesota Multiphasic Personality Inventory—2 (MMPI–2), 4
administration of, 20
development of, 10–11
Masculinity/Femininity Scale on, 76
MMPI–2–RF profiles on, 12
normative sample for MMPI–2–RF and, 24
protocol validity measures on, 29
Psychoticism Scale on, 64
Restructured Clinical Scales for, 11–12
scores on, 24
Minnesota Multiphasic Personality Inventory—2—Restructured Form (MMPI–2–RF), 3. *See also specific topics*
development of, 12
dimensional framework in, 3–4, 12–14
MMPI vs., 3
organization of, 7, 9
psychometric considerations with, 14–17, 15*t*
psychopathology assessment model used in, 3, 8*f*
scales of, 15*t*
settings for, 111–113
Minnesota Multiphasic Personality Inventory—Adolescent—Restructured Form (MMPI–A–RF), 4, 20
Minnesota Normals group, 9–10
Mistrust (CAT-PD), 75
MLS. See Malaise scale
MMPI. *See* Minnesota Multiphasic Personality Inventory
MMPI–2. *See* Minnesota Multiphasic Personality Inventory—2
MMPI–2–RF. *See* Minnesota Multiphasic Personality Inventory—2—Restructured Form
MMPI–2–RF Interpretation Worksheet. *See* Interpretation Worksheet, MMPI–2–RF
MMPI–2–RF Manual for Administration, Scoring, and Interpretation (Ben-Porath & Tellegen), 4, 5, 19, 88, 107
MMPI–2–RF Technical Manual (Tellegen & Ben-Porath), 4, 16
MMPI–A–RF (Minnesota Multiphasic Personality Inventory—Adolescent—Restructured Form), 4, 20
Modalities, standard, 21–22
Mood-stabilizing medication, 69, 70
Multiple Specific Fears scale (*MSF*), 51, 59–60

N

Narcissistic personality disorder, 69, 74
Narrative report
for case example, 108, 109*e*
and Interpretation Worksheet, 82
preparation of, 86–88
Narrow scales, 3, 4, 45
National Institute of Mental Health (NIMH), 3, 13
Negative Emotionality/Neuroticism–Revised scale (*NEGE-r*)
breadth of, 51
in case example, 103–104, 106
content and interpretation of, 60–61
Negative emotions. *See* Dysfunctional Negative Emotions scale (*RC7*)
Negative information, 61
Negative response bias, 33
NEGE-r. See Negative Emotionality/Neuroticism–Revised scale
Neo-Kraepelinian categorical model, 87
Neurological Complaints scale (*NUC*), 46, 47, 49
Neurological disorders, 63
Neuropsychological evaluation, 50
Neuroticism, 60, 61. *See also* Negative Emotionality/Neuroticism–Revised scale (NEGE-r)
NFC. See Inefficacy scale
Nichols, D. S., 10
NIMH (National Institute of Mental Health), 3, 13
Nonacquiescence, 32, 41
Noncompliance, treatment, 66, 67, 71
Nongendered norms, 24
Nonresponding (term), 30, 41. *See also* Content nonresponsiveness
Normative group, 24
Notes, in narrative report, 87
NUC. See Neurological Complaints scale

O

Obsessive–compulsive disorder, 57
Occupational settings, 112
"Official" interpretive statements, 5
Oppositional defiant disorders, 65
Outpatient comparison group, 27
Overreporting of psychopathology, 32–37
and case example, 90
defined, 30
fixed responding and, 42
Infrequent Psychopathology Responses measure, 34–35

Overreporting of psychopathology, *continued*
- Infrequent Responses measure, 33–34
- Infrequent Somatic Responses measure, 35–36
- intentional, 33
- interpretation procedure to evaluate, 79, 82
- and psychometric considerations with MMPI–2–RF, 16
- random responding and, 42
- research on, 29
- Response Bias measure, 36–38
- score patterns indicating, 42–43
- Symptom Validity measure, 36
- unintentional, 33, 43

P

Pain, chronic, 111
Pain management techniques, 49
Paranoia Scale (MMPI), 9, 62
Paranoid disorders, 63
Parental assessments, 112
Passivity, 54, 55, 74. *See also* Interpersonal Passivity scale (*IPP*)
Pattern analysis, with MMPI, 10
Pearson Assessments, 21, 22, 27
Pearson Clinical Assessments website, 12, 26, 79
Persecutory ideas, 62–63. *See also* Ideas of Persecution scale (*RC6*)
Personal injury litigation, 112
Personality, five-factor model of, 60, 64, 65, 71
Personality disorders, 61, 64, 70, 73
Personality Psychopathology Five Scales (PSY-5), 12
- Aggressiveness–Revised scale in, 65, 70
- in case example, 90, 96*f*, 103–104
- development of, 10
- and dimensional model of psychopathology, 13
- Disconstraint–Revised scale in, 65, 71
- in interpretation procedure, 84
- interpreting scores on, 81
- Introversion/Low Positive Emotionality–Revised scale in, 56
- item overlap and, 17
- Negative Emotionality/Neuroticism–Revised scale in, 60
- Psychoticism–Revised scale in, 61, 64
- on Score Report, 25

Phobias, 59, 60, 75
Physical complaints. *See* Somatic/Cognitive domain
Physically aggressive behavior, 69
Police Candidate Interpretive Report, 25, 112
Positive adjustment, 43
Positive emotionality. *See* Introversion/Low Positive Emotionality–Revised scale (*INTR-r*)
Positive emotions. *See* Low Positive Emotions scale (*RC2*)
Positive malingering, 37
Posttraumatic stress disorder, 58
Prior testing, with client, 20
Protocol validity. *See also* Protocol Validity Scales
- assessing, with MMPI–2–RF, 7
- importance of, 40–41
- instructions related to, 23
- MMPI and MMPI–2 measures of, 29

Protocol Validity Scales, 12, 29–43
- and Aggression scale, 69
- in case example, 90, 105
- for content nonresponsiveness threats, 30–32
- interpreting scores on, 79–80, 82
- issues from, on narrative report, 86
- for overreporting threats, 32–37
- and psychometric considerations with MMPI–2–RF, 14
- score patterns on, 40–43
- on Score Report, 25
- and Somatic/Cognitive domain, 46
- *T*-scores for, 24, 25
- for underreporting threats, 37–40

PSY-5. *See* Personality Psychopathology Five Scales
PSYC (Psychoticism Scale), 64
Psychasthenia category (MMPI), 9
Psychological Assessment Series (APA), 4–5
Psychological distress, 52
Psychological report, full, 85–86, 108
Psychopathic Deviate Scale (MMPI), 9, 71
Psychopathology
- categorical model of, 9, 12, 13, 87
- dimensional model of, 13–14
- overreporting of. *See* Overreporting of psychopathology
- and scores on overreporting scales, 43
- underreporting of. *See* Underreporting of psychopathology

Psychopathology assessment model
- MMPI–2–RF in, 3, 8*f*, 87
- paradigm shift in, 12–14
- Somatic/Cognitive domain in, 46

Psychosis, 61
Psychotic disorders, 61, 63
Psychoticism, 61, 64
Psychoticism–Revised scale (*PSYC-r*)
- in case example, 106
- content and interpretation of, 64
- in interpretation procedure, 85
- as PSY-5 scale, 61
- and Thought Dysfunction scale, 62

Psychoticism Scale (*PSYC*), 64
PSYC-r. *See* Psychoticism–Revised scale

Q

Q-global platform, 21
Q Local platform, 22

Qualified professional, test administration by, 19–20
Questions, test takers', 22–23

R

Random responding, 30, 31, 41–42
Raw score, 23, 24
RBS measure. *See* Response Bias measure
RC1. *See* Somatic Complaints scale
RC2. *See* Low Positive Emotions scale
RC3. *See* Cynicism scale
RC4. *See* Antisocial Behavior scale
RC6. *See* Ideas of Persecution scale
RC7. *See* Dysfunctional Negative Emotions scale
RC8. *See* Aberrant Experiences scale
RC9. *See* Hypomanic Activation scale
RCd. *See* Demoralization scale
RC Scales. *See* Restructured Clinical Scales
RDoC (Research Domain Criteria) project, 3, 13
Reading level, of client, 20–21
Reference list (Interpretive Report), 26
Relationship, therapeutic, 63, 73, 76
Reliability, 16
Reporting. *See also* Narrative report; Score Report
  full psychological report, 85–86, 108
  options and procedures for, 25–27
  over-. *See* Overreporting of psychopathology
  self-report instruments, 19
  under-. *See* Underreporting of psychopathology
Research Domain Criteria (RDoC) project, 3, 13
Responding
  fixed, 30, 41, 42
  inconsistent, 38, 41–42
  random, 30, 31, 40–42
Response Bias measure (*RBS*)
  in case example, 90
  content and interpretation of, 36, 37, 38*t*
  in interpretation procedure, 79
  random responding and, 42
  and Somatic/Cognitive domain, 46
  and Somatic/Cognitive domain scores, 49
Responsiveness, 16. *See also* Content nonresponsiveness
Restandardization Committee, MMPI, 11
Restructured Clinical (RC) Scales. *See also specific scales*
  in case example, 90, 93*f*, 103, 104
  development of, 11–12
  in Externalizing domain, 65
  and Higher-Order scales, 62
  in Internalizing domain, 50
  in Interpersonal Functioning domain, 72
  interpreting scores on, 80, 85
  item overlap and, 17
  and MMPI–2, 4
  on Score Report, 25
  in Thought Dysfunction domain, 61
Rudeness (CAT-PD), 73
Rumination, excessive, 57

S

S (Superlative Self-Presentation measure), 29
SAV. *See* Social Avoidance scale
Schizoaffective disorder, 69
Schizoid personality disorder, 75, 76
Schizophrenia, paranoid type, 64
Schizophrenia category (MMPI), 9, 61
Score Report, 5
  Aberrant Experiences score on, 63
  Aggression score on, 69
  for case example, 90, 91*f*–98*f*
  computer-assisted, 28
  features of, 25–26
  Helplessness/Hopelessness score on, 53
  Ideas of Persecution score on, 62
  and interpretation procedure, 80, 81
  preparing Interpretation Worksheet from, 82, 83
  Substance Abuse score on, 67
  Suicidal/Death Ideation score on, 52
Scores-by-domain report, 25
Scoring
  computer-assisted, 23–24, 28
  hand, 23–24, 28
  and modality, 21
  options and procedures for, 23–25
Second pass review
  in case example, 104–108
  conducting, 82–86
  and Score Report, 25
  in two-pass approach, 77
Seizure disorders, 111
Self-control, 66, 67
Self-Doubt scale (*SFD*), 51, 54, 103
Self-efficacy, 54
Self-esteem, low, 54
Self-harm, 52
Self-referential delusions, 62
Self-reliance, 54–55
Self-report instruments, 19
Sellbom, M., 29, 112
SFD. *See* Self-Doubt scale
Shyness scale (*SHY*)
  breadth of, 72
  in case example, 103, 107
  content and interpretation of, 75
  and Disaffiliativeness score, 75
  and Neurological Complaints score, 49
  and Social Avoidance score, 74
  and Somatic Complaints score, 47
Simple phobias, 59
Social anxiety, 74
Social Avoidance scale (*SAV*)
  breadth of, 72
  in case example, 103, 107

Social Avoidance scale, *continued*
content and interpretation of, 74–75
and Disaffiliativeness scale, 75
Social disengagement, 56
Social Introversion Scale (MMPI), 9
Social phobia, 75
Social withdrawal, 75
Social Withdrawal (CAT-PD), 74, 75
Somatic/Cognitive domain, 3, 4
in assessment model, 8*f*, 9
in case example, 90, 94*f*, 105
Cognitive Complaints scale, 49
description of, 46
Gastrointestinal Complaints scale, 48
Head Pain Complaints scale, 48–49
in interpretation procedure, 80, 83
Malaise scale, 47
Neurological Complaints scale, 49
and psychometric considerations with MMPI–2–RF, 16
scales within, 46–51
on Score Report, 25
Somatic Complaints scale, 46–47
and Symptom Validity scale, 36
Somatic complaints, overreporting of, 35, 43
Somatic Complaints scale (*RC1*)
breadth of, 46
in case example, 103, 105
content and interpretation of, 46–47
in interpretation procedure, 83
Somatoform disorder, 33, 47–49
Specialized questionnaires, administration of MMPI–2–RF with, 112
Specific phobias, 60
Specific Problems (SP) Scales, 12
in case example, 90, 103
in Externalizing domain, 65
in interpretation procedure, 80, 84, 85
item overlap and, 17
Malaise scale as, 46
on Score Report, 25
Spinal surgery, 111
SP Scales. *See* Specific Problems Scales
Standard deviation, 27
Standardization group, MMPI, 10
Standardized administration procedures, 19, 22–23
Standardized instructions, 22–23
Standard scores, 24–25
Stress-reduction interventions, 48
Stress-related disorders, 57
Stress/Worry scale (*STW*)
breadth of, 51
in case example, 103, 106
content and interpretation of, 57
STW. See Stress/Worry scale
Substance Abuse scale (*SUB*)
and Activation scale, 70
and Antisocial Behavior scale, 66
breadth of, 65
in case example, 105
content and interpretation of, 67–68
as Critical Scale, 16
in interpretation procedure, 81
and Juvenile Conduct Problems scale, 67
marijuana use and scores on, 104
on Score Report, 26
Substance use, 63
Substance-use related disorders, 66, 68
Substantive Scales, 45–76
in case example, 103, 105–107
Externalizing domain, 64–71
and Interest Scales, 76
Internalizing domain, 50–61
Interpersonal Functioning domain, 71–76
and interpersonal relationships, 71
interpreting scores on, 80–81, 83–86
organization of, 7, 9
and Protocol Validity Scales, 30, 38, 41
Somatic/Cognitive domain, 46–50
Thought Dysfunction domain, 61–64
T-scores for, 25
Suicidal/Death Ideation scale (*SUI*)
breadth of, 51
in case example, 103, 104
content and interpretation of, 52–53
as Critical Scale, 16
in interpretation procedure, 80
on Score Report, 26
Suicidal ideation, 54
Suicide, risk for, 53
Superlative Self-Presentation measure (*S*), 29
Supplementary Scales (MMPI), 10
Symptom Validity measure (*FBS-r*)
in case example, 90
content and interpretation of, 36, 37*t*
in interpretation procedure, 79
overreporting and scores on, 43
random responding and, 42
and Somatic/Cognitive domain scores, 46, 47, 49, 50

T

Tags, in Interpretive Report, 26
Tellegen, A., 4, 5, 11, 16, 19, 29, 88, 107
Ternes, M. S., 29
Testability, client, 20–21
Test of Memory Malingering, 36
Test-taking attitude, 29, 30. *See also* Protocol Validity Scales
THD. See Thought Dysfunction scale
Therapeutic relationship, 63, 73, 76
Thinking, disordered, 63

Thought Dysfunction domain, 3
in assessment model, 8*f*, 9
in case example, 106
description of, 61
and psychometric considerations with MMPI–2–RF, 16
scales within, 61–64
Thought Dysfunction scale (*THD*), 14
breadth of, 61
in case example, 103, 106
content and interpretation of, 61–62
in interpretation procedure, 85
and Psychoticism–Revised scale, 64
Three-factor model for internalizing dysfunction, 50, 84
Toomey, A., 29
Training, for test administrator, 21
Treatment Considerations section (Interpretation Worksheet), 107–108
TRIN (True Response Inconsistency), 29
TRIN-r. See True Response Inconsistency measure
True (response)
answering both *false* and, 31
as fixed response, 30, 32, 42
True Response Inconsistency (*TRIN*), 29
True Response Inconsistency measure (*TRIN-r*)
in case example, 90
content and interpretation of, 32, 33*t*
cutoff score for, 41
and fixed responding, 30, 42
in interpretation procedure, 79
research on, 29
scoring of, 28
Trust, lack of, 73
T-score
and Anxiety score, 58
calculating, 24
for case example, 97*f*
and Suicidal/Death Ideation score, 52
and True Response Inconsistency measure, 32
Uniform, 24
Two-pass interpretation approach, 3, 45, 77. *See also* Interpretation of MMPI–2–RF

U

Uncommon Virtues measure (*L-r*)
in case example, 90
content and interpretation of, 38, 39*t*
fixed responding and, 42
in interpretation procedure, 80
random responding and, 42
and Substantive Scales, 38
underreporting and scores on, 43
Uncooperative test takers, 42
Underreporting of psychopathology
and Cannot Say measure, 31
and case example, 90
defined, 30
fixed responding and, 42
intentional, 43
interpretation procedure to evaluate, 80, 82
and psychometric considerations with MMPI–2–RF, 16
random responding and, 42
research on, 29
scales for, 37–40
score patterns indicating, 43
unintentional, 43
Uniform *T* score, 24
Unintentional overreporting, 33, 43
Unintentional random responding, 42
Unintentional underreporting, 43
University of Minnesota Hospitals, 9, 10
University of Minnesota Press, 12, 16, 79

V

Validity
adjustment. *See* Adjustment Validity measure (*K-r*)
content, 5
criterion, 5
independent, 84
of MMPI–2–RF, 16–17
protocol, 7, 23, 29, 40–41. *See also* Protocol Validity Scales
symptom. *See* Symptom Validity measure (*FBS-r*)
Variable Response Inconsistency (*VRIN*), 29
Variable Response Inconsistency measure (*VRIN-r*)
in case example, 90
content and interpretation of, 31, 32*t*
cutoff score for, 41
and fixed responding, 42
in interpretation procedure, 79
and random responding, 30, 41–42
research on, 29
scoring of, 28
Veterans Affairs samples, comparison group, 27
Virtuousness, 38
VRIN (Variable Response Inconsistency), 29
VRIN-r. See Variable Response Inconsistency measure

W

Watson, D., 13
Wechsler tests, 19, 23
Welsh, G. S., 10
Withdrawal, social, 75
Word Memory Test, 36
World Health Organization, 108. *See also International Classification of Diseases* (ICD)
Worry, excessive, 57. *See also* Stress/Worry scale (*STW*)
Wygant, D., 29, 35, 50

About the Author

David M. McCord, PhD, is a professor of clinical psychology at Western Carolina University in Cullowhee, North Carolina. He received a BA in psychology from Duke University in 1972, an MA in clinical psychology from Western Carolina University in 1979, and a PhD in clinical psychology from the University of Alabama in 1984, where he studied with Dr. Raymond Fowler. He completed his predoctoral internship year in the School of Medicine, University of North Carolina at Chapel Hill, in 1984, mentored by Dr. Charles S. Newmark. His publications and professional presentations focus generally on personality assessment and personality theory, with a primary focus on the Minnesota Multiphasic Personality Inventory—2—Restructured Clinical Scales and the Minnesota Multiphasic Personality Inventory—2—Restructured Form. He serves on the editorial board of *Psychological Assessment* and is a frequent ad hoc reviewer for other journals.